Tantra,
Yoga of Ecstasy

The Sadhaka's Guide to
Kundalini and the Left-Hand Path

by

Leigh Hurley & Phillip Hurley

Maithuna Publications

2012

Tantra, Yoga of Ecstasy:
The Sadhaka's Guide to Kundalini and the Left-Hand Path

Series: The Sadhaka's Guide, Volume 1

Maithuna Publications is an imprint of:

Good Idea Creative Services
324 Minister Hill Road
Wheelock VT 05851 USA

ISBN 978-0-9837847-2-2

Library of Congress Control Number: 2012936015

Library of Congress subject headings:

Tantrism~Handbooks, manuals, etc.
Tantrism~Rituals
Tantrism~Psychology
Yoga~Tantrism
Kundalini
Kundalini~Handbooks, manuals, etc.

Authors' website:

www.tantrayoga.us

Contents

Contents

Preface

Tantra is an ancient discipline with deep cosmic roots. Tantric principles are honored in temples across India, where the Shiva lingam and the Shakti yoni are the bindu, the centerpoint of the temples and their rituals.

These temple symbols bring us back to first principles, not in an academic sense, but in a feeling way that engages all of our senses. We are led to bindu by the manifestation of these first principles in our lives at all levels.

Every movement in time and space is ritual for the Tantric sadhaka, and every moment is a moment of transmutation, of alchemy.

The lingam and yoni, and the desire that brings them together, is the beginning of all humans and all things physical. The sexual act, born of sensual discovery, is the key to transmutation. One can try to hide from this fact of life, deny it or dishonor it by considering it a sin. But, to evolve and grow into spiritual adulthood, each of us must understand the energies that brought us here and have made us as we are. With this understanding, we can perform the alchemy, the transmutation that will lead us more quickly to moksha, liberation from ignorance.

The words in this book are a mantra that follows the path of kundalini, rising up to the summit of Mt. Meru, the sahasrara chakra. As the words enter your consciousness, toss them onto the fires of wisdom as a sacrifice, let them dissolve, rise up to Mt. Meru, be clarified and cycle back downward to become your own.

अ

अ

Note to the reader

This book includes a lot of Sanskrit terms. We have tried to be as explanatory as possible without over-burdening the text, and have included a glossary for your reference.

While not strictly necessary, it is a very worthwhile endeavor for the sadhaka, the Tantric practitioner, to learn some of these terms. Sanskrit is a very sophisticated language in the realm of the exploration of human consciousness and the practice of yoga, and many words for important concepts have no real equivalents in English.

Origins and Influence of Tantra Yoga

The origins of Tantra can be traced with some certainty to the northeast portion of India in what are now the states of Assam, Bengal, Bihar and Orissa. Various Tantric writings such as the *Bukyasarvaja, Manjusthanubakalpa* and *Hevajratantra* began to appear in this region around the 4th century CE. The yoga of eroticism seems to have flourished in this region until the 13th century when the Moslems sacked India.

Many temples of that era were constructed in a Tantric style, incorporating a variety of erotic art sculptures into their architecture. At the center of each, within the inner sanctum, is a male phallus symbol (lingam) inserted in a female genital symbol (yoni).

In the very heart of India lies the small town of Khajuraho which hosts a complex of 85 temples, 22 of which are in some repair for viewing. Khajuraho was a center for Tantra as is shown in the facades of the buildings which are covered with sculptures of copulating couples and delightful orgies. The sculptures are extremely explicit.

These temples are a major source of embarrassment for many East Indians whose modern culture is quite conservative - only recently were movies allowed to show couples kissing. The most common explanation presently given for the wild eroticism of the temple art is that the temples depicted life in all its aspects, "good and bad." One of Mahatma Ghandi's colleagues even stood up in Parliment and suggested destroying the sculptures lining the temple walls by pouring concrete over them. Fortunately, that didn't happen.

Sculpture on a temple
in Khajuraho

Much of the lore about Tantra is hard to validate. One legend is that Padmasambhave, a son of Indrabhuti (King of Orissa), was responsible for introducing Tantra into Tibet, and founded the Red Hat sect of Lamaism. It is believed that after the Moslem invasion of India, Tantra went underground in India, but flourished in modified forms openly in Tibet, Nepal, and the Himalayan regions in general. Many Tantric practices were adopted by priests of the Bon religion in the Himalayas, and Bon oral tradition supposedly continues in an unbroken chain to this present day.

The real historical origins of Tantra remain obscure. What is apparent however, is that as Tantra flourished, some of its practices became incorporated into a variety of religious sects in the region such as the Aghoris, Nathists, Shaivites and Shaktas. None of these sects represents the whole of Tantra, although each sect claims to have the original seed teachings, according to their lights.

Within some of these groups are further subdivisions. In the Shaivite school there are the Trika in Kashmir and the Shaiva Siddhanta in the southern parts of the country. Among the Shaktas there are three major subdivisions – Kaula, Mishra, and Samaya.

The seed teachings of Tantra are known as *agamas* – revelations or authentic utterances. Some have a divine person attributed as their source; generally Shiva, Shakti, or Vishnu. In western India there are also agamas from other deities such as the Ganapatyas and the Sauras. All of these comprise the five basic groups collectively called *Pancha Upasakas*.

These include the *Kaula Agama,* which stresses *artha* (material prosperity) and *kama* (enjoyment); the *Mishra Agama* which stresses action, and is concerned with fulfillment of dharma, moral development; and the *Samaya Agama,* which is focused on developing a more inward approach to *moksha*, liberation.

Vedic deities, language and philosophy have been incorporated into Tantra. Similarly, the yoga of Patanjali and other forms of yoga (all heavily influenced by Tantra) have been grafted into the Vedas and vedic practice.

Down through the ages there appear to have been attempts by some followers of the Tantra *sastra* to legitimize their discipline in the view of vedic culture. The attempt at best has not fooled anyone, least of all, true Tantrics.

When all is said and done, Tantra is at best considered a child without a home. The nature of the practice places it absolutely at odds with entrenched cultural institutions.

Tantra, yoga, and Buddhism all formed as reactions against the stranglehold the brahmin caste had on Indian culture with its rigid class system, and subjugation of women.

Vivian Worthington mentions in *History of Yoga:*

"All the Hindu Tantras were opposed to caste, sex discrimination and sati - the custom which required the widow to throw herself on the dead husband's funeral pyre at his cremation."

Tantra has been a powerful voice for equality among people since its inception, holding to the belief that liberation of self does not permit the subjugation of others. To subjugate others is to subjugate the self.

Even in its early stages, women were allowed to be teachers of Tantra, and Tantric teachers spoke out, for instance, against the caste system and sati. All castes were welcome within the ranks of

Tantra, while brahmanic India would not allow such blasphemous outrages to exist within its very tightly class-ruled ranks. Even access to the Vedas (the ancient sacred texts of India) was restricted by the brahmins to the three higher castes - the brahmins, kshatriyas and the vaishyas.

Although some Tantric sects claim allegiance to the Vedas, at the same time they feel free to interpret the Vedas for their own era. There is a great gulf between the practice of Veda and yoga. The main interest expressed in the Vedas is ritual, sacrifice and the myriad of details surrounding these. Yoga is only concerned with the psycho-spiritual aspects of its adherents.

There is speculation that much of Tantra and yoga is really a remnant of the culture that flourished at places such as Mohenjo Daro and Harappa. Although fascinating, to the Tantric such speculation is of little importance. Tantrics assert that revelation derived from individual *sadhana* is the key. The history of the practice should be left to the scholars to debate.

In the early part of the 20th century, western interest in Tantra was kindled with the publication of several books by Sir John Woodruff, aka Arthur Avalon. His publication of the *Mahanirvana Tantra* and other works, although limited in scope, revealed some of the more ascetic practices of some schools of Tantra, with a heavy emphasis on *mantra,* the secret magical language of India. Woodruff's works are interesting, but do not shed much light on the philosophy of Tantra - the language is archaic and dusty, and not very revealing.

For the Tantric, the origin of Tantra is within each practitioner. It is everywhere within everyone at all times:

> *"What is here is there;*
> *what is not here is not there"*
> *- Visvasara Tantra.*

Tantra yoga padas

The texts on which the classical study of Tantra is based are referred to as the Tantra shastra. They delineate a total approach for the sadhaka, intended to lead to moksha (liberation). Tantra shastra divides the practice into four *padas* (parts): *jnana, kriya, yoga* and *charya* pada.

Jnana pada is the intellectual study of the metaphysical and philosophical base for the system, including the study of various agamas.

Kriya pada consists of communal practice which is, for the Tantric, the pancha makara or 5M ritual.

Yoga pada is the practice of various techniques to raise the kundalini.

Charya pada is the practice of each individual according to their talents and insights. It is dependent on the *guna* that predominates in the personality of the practitioner. The three gunas are *tamas, sattwa,* and *rajas*. The individual in which the tamasic nature is dominant is called *pasu*; with the sattwic dominant, *deva*; and with the rajasic dominant, *vira*. These three types require different approaches to the practice of Tantra. The tamasic person is very physical, connected to the realm of earth and responds readily to basic needs. The rajasic person is full of vigor and vitality and is impetuous in action, emotional. The sattwic person is generally led by light of intellectual reasoning.

Tantra is a wholistic discipline designed to balance the mental, emotional and physical spheres of each practitioner. The individual practice (sadhana) develops and changes over time to incorporate the other two gunas as the practitioner becomes more balanced.

There are posited two paths in Tantra, *vama marga*, often called the left-hand path, and *daksina marga*, often called the right-hand path. The distinction is that vama marga incorporates our sexual nature into the ritual discipline: sexual intercourse takes place in the pancha makara ritual. For the daksina marga it does not, except in a symbolic way.

Practitioners of vama marga are called *vamacharins* (magicians). This path is the core discipline of Tantra, whereas daksina marga is reserved for those who either by age, physical debilitation, or preference, choose to only symbolize the sexual act. However, those who practice daksina marga must accept the validity of the left-hand path. Tantra involves the whole of human nature in the discipline. If someone wished to practice daksina marga out of fear of sex, or based upon a moralist system that denied the spiritual base of the act of sex, such practice would not be daksina marga.

The term left-hand path as applied to Tantra came about because at one time left-handed people were considered sinister and evil. Very few people do actually participate in the path of the left hand because they are not able to stand up to the strength of popular moral injunctions against such activities. To perform *maithuna,* (the sexual act) for pleasure has often been considered a condemnable sinister and evil act, so vama marga has been and still is usually considered morally incorrect in most cultural contexts. From a Christian point of view, practitioners of vama marga would be considered a satanic cult.

However, Tantra is not a religion. It is a spiritual practice, a technique for achieving *vidya,* meaning greater understanding, or enlightenment. Tantra's root philosophy is that *kama,* the fulfillment of sensual desires; *artha,* prosperity; *dharma,* spiritual and moral duty; and *moksha,* liberation are all one. The Tantric rises by means of human nature, not by rejecting it, and the sadhaka gains awareness that goes beyond popular morality and asceticism. From the Tantric perspective, conventional morality and asceticism are intended to keep those of lesser understanding in line and prevent them from hurting each other, until they achieve enough spiritual maturity and awareness of the consequences of their actions that they can truly be responsible for themselves. Conventional moral aphorisms and religions belong to spiritual childhood.

The initiation into spiritual adulthood is demonstrated in pancha makara (the ritual of the five elements), which flouts conventional morality. Wine, meat and sexual intercourse are freely enjoyed in a group context.

Beef was usually included in the pancha makara because the cow is sacred in Indian culture. To eat beef was and is considered sacrilegious. Also, to show affection in public was and is considered shameful. In this social context, one can only imagine how vile the act of communal sexual intercourse, and the whole pancha makara must have appeared to the general population.

This should convey the radical nature of Tantric practice and how far out it really was compared to indigenous cultural norms. It is important to get a feel for the discipline within the context of the culture which spawned it, and within the cultures it has passed through, in order to understand it.

Tantric sadhana is intended to challenge cultural convention and institutional norms, physically, mentally, and emotionally in order to liberate the sadhaka from *avidya*, the limited perspective imposed by our personal and social group *samskaras*.

So, the practice of Tantra is not merely internal meditation. Tantra touches every fibre of the human being. It is a path of action, it is life oriented, and is a social path as the sadhaka realizes that he or she is a part of a larger whole. It becomes apparent to the sadhaka that the self must commune with the "not self," meaning others, to balance the forces of karma.

The core of Tantric practice is to merge polar opposites with the dedicated intent to transcend the limited vision which our *samskaras* (karmic tendencies) afford us. In the merging and balance of polarity, *bindu*, a state of bliss, is created. Achieving bindu is the goal of performing the three great Tantric rituals: pancha makara, Shiva/Shakti meditation, and *bhuta-shuddhi* (refinement of the tattwas).

Pancha makara brings together the feeling of pleasure with the object or quality which gives the pleasure - thus joining the one who desires and the object of desire.

Similarly, in Shiva/Shakti meditation, the female sadhaka contemplates the Shiva, and the male sadhaka contemplates the Shakti, to understand and integrate the opposite polarity. The contemplator becomes one with the object of contemplation.

In bhuta-shuddhi, known also as raising kundalini, the two seemingly opposing poles of existence, the muladhara chakra and the sahasrara chakra, are connected and merged into one. All of these concepts and practices are maithuna or "bringing together," a merging which produces the *amrita* (nectar of the gods) and enlightenment.

The specific components of Tantric rituals and practices vary widely. Each school of Tantra has its preferred method and mode. However, all use mantra; mudra; images to house the soul or knowledge of deities; emblems, such as the yoni and lingam to represent cosmic principles; and yantras (linear figures that due to their shape and design evoke and invoke the powers and knowledge of the cosmos). All of these devices are templates, each with their own character, meaning and power.

Each form, each sound, each color, each substance incorporated by the Tantric into the ritual of maithuna, no matter what level, has a magical effect upon the consciousness of the participant. Tantra is first and foremost a magical discipline.

The key to Tantric ritual and practice is that every act is dedicated to enlightenment and moksa (liberation). In Tantric philosophy, any action performed with dedication is an act which will produce the results intended. Certain acts are prescribed because they have a primal physical connection to us and our existence. For instance, imbibing food and drink, and the sexual act itself are perhaps the most powerful components of our being because they are the most basic of our needs and desires.

The Tantric realizes that the whole of what is called civilization is based on fulfilling these needs: to feed, shelter and clothe ourselves, and to commune with others socially. All economies are built upon these needs. Humans seek comfort, because comfort is pleasure. No one seeks pain as an end in itself.

Tantra starts with these obvious primal human needs and understands that all acts are in themselves revelatory in nature when the person acting comprehends that they ARE revelatory in nature. The small pleasures we enjoy, are, to the Tantric, bits of amrita (nectar of the gods), revelations and transcendent connections to be touched and lived. They have great transformative power; the power to transmute our lives, to change karma and rid ourselves of the samskaras which rule our unenlightened lives.

To take part in a Tantric ritual is to perform alchemy. In sexual union, no matter at what level, the *sahasrara chakra* combines with the *muladhara chakra* to transmute matter, so it is no mistake that the European alchemists of the Middle Ages used sexual symbolism quite graphically to depict their operations.

Elements of Tantra have passed down through the ages through a variety of cultures. One can easily see Tantric roots in Indian alchemy (*rasayana*), Taoist alchemy, and European alchemy.

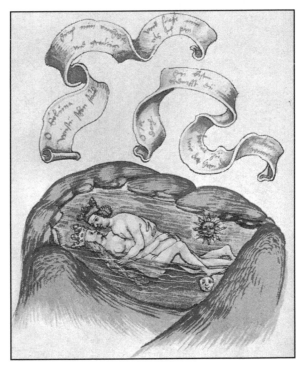

The perfect solution of solar and lunar opposites, part of an alchemical process as depicted in *Rosarium Philosophorum*.

Influence of Tantra

The Crusades brought Europeans into contact with cultures who had knowledge of Tantra. Some of this esoteric knowledge reached Europe via sea and overland trade routes, and brought forth European alchemy.

The goal of the European alchemist was the Philosophers Stone, which had the power to transmute matter and conscious awareness. To produce this stone, the power of Shiva-Shakti in sexual union was necessary, as is shown in such texts as *Rosarium Philosophorum* and *Donum Dei*. These and many other texts show male and female in sexual intercourse. The combination of polar opposites dissolves the essential nature of each.

Kama, desire, here is understood as the universal solvent, which pulls the opposites together and allows them to merge. Alchemical texts state that without this "corruption" of the ego, in other words, dissolution of the individuated opposites to a basic state, there can be no generation. In union, the couple form what the alchemists call dark matter or nigredo, a pristine state from which the perfect child is produced. In Tantric or alchemical terms, the perfect child represents not a physical child, but a state of consciousness which is informed by *sunyata* or *akasha*, the void. Two halves are combined to produce a whole, to perfect wisdom and knowledge. The whole is the *merudanda*, the center of the universe, the apex of the creative matrix.

European alchemy, and its Tantric base, heavily influenced Carl Jung's system of psychology. His philosophy revolves around the union of polar opposites, female and male principles. Freud's system of psychotherapy also contains elements of Tantra, in that at some level he recognized the transmutation of energy from the *id* to the *ego* and *superego* (terms and concepts that he postulated to explain his observations). Thus, Tantra can be found at the roots even of present day psychotherapy.

अं

The agamas, the sources, for a Tantric today are not only what are considered the classical agamas, but also a vast body of literature, art and practices which has been incorporated into many cultures and esoteric systems.

अ

Hymn of Creation
Rig Veda – 1500 BC (or older)

Then even nothingness was not, nor existence
There was no air then, nor the heavens beyond it.
What covered it? Where was it? In whose keeping?
Was there then cosmic water, in depths unfathomed?

Then there was neither death nor immortality,
nor was there then the torch of night and day.
The One breathed windlessly and self-sustaining.
There was One then, and there was no other.

At first there was only darkness wrapped in darkness.
All this was only unillumined water.
That One which came to be, enclosed in nothing,
arose at last, born of the power of heat.
In the beginning desire descended on it -
that was the primal seed, born of the mind.

The sages who have searched their hearts with wisdom
know that which is, is kin to what is not.
And they have stretched their cord across the void,
and known what was above and what below.

Seminal powers made fertile mighty forces.
Below was strength, and over it was impulse.
But after all, who knows, and who can say
Whence it all came, and how creation happened?

The gods themselves are later than creation,
so who knows truly whence it has arisen?
Whence all creation had its origin,
he, whether he fashioned it or whether he did not,
he, who surveys it all from the highest heaven,
he knows - or maybe even he does not know.

Tantric Philosophy

One of the meanings of the word Tantra is "to weave." A closely-viewed tapestry seems like many different threads. Stepping back, unity and recurring patterns are perceived. Pull on one strand and many other strands are affected, some in distant parts of the cloth. We are all at once the weaver, and the tapestry, and the strands.

Tantra is a path of discovery that leads to *moksha* (liberation) from *avidya* (ignorance). It is a process of contemplating the *tattwas*, the creative changing aspects of the coming together of Shiva and Shakti, that is, the tapestry created by the universal polarity and all its permutations.

In weaving, the warp and weft produce a fabric, a whole. In all polarities, Shiva/Shakti, warp/weft, the individuals are all parts of the same larger wholeness, the same stuff , but they are differentiated and defined by their relationship to one another. Any polarity pair exists as an integral relationship - one polarity defines the other, and would not exist without the other, and vice versa.

This includes the self, or "I" (*aham*), and the not-self or "this" (*idam*). Contemplation of dynamic polarity produces a state of awareness in which idam and aham combine. Within this state of awareness comes the realization that all is one (*para-samvit*). This is expressed in the **Visvasara Tantra** by the phrase, "What is here is there; what is not here is no there."

The experience of ecstatic union is the goal of Tantra sadhana - to deeply feel the connectedness of all things. Ecstatic union is the result of the *maha mudra*, literally, "the great gesture," which is *maithuna*, the great sexual act.

In the uniting of polar opposites, individualness dissolves, replaced by a third component: consciousness of a wholeness which has within it the keys to liberation from *avidya* (ignorance) and freedom from the bondage of *maya* (illusion).

Liberation from ignorance, the experience of wholeness, allows the sadhaka to move freely with the light of knowledge and wisdom, amidst oceans of seemingly complex diversity.

Matter & form become enlightened

For the Tantric, all is Tantra. Every movement through time and space, and every interaction of each and every particle is an act of maithuna which liberates energy from matter.

It is the nature of biological creatures to liberate themselves by releasing and spending their energies in a grand scheme of sexual union to produce the *amrita* of bliss, knowledge and wisdom and wholeness. Thus, ask a Tantric who does Tantra, and they will reply "everything and everybody, whether they know it or not. It is what is!"

The Tantric sadhana, the path to enlightenment, is embedded in matter and form. The interactions of forms tell a story that constantly in-forms us. We are constantly learning and constantly realizing; and the Tantric knows that all matter and embodied beings will be liberated sooner or later. All walk the path due to our very nature and the nature of the cosmos. We are enlightened and informed with every action and movement.

For instance, the sciences of physics, chemistry, biology, sociology, and psychology are all manifestations of one principle. Each of these disciplines is simply a qualitative pigeon-holing of the same phenomenon at different levels of structure. That is, the laws of physics do not become inoperative just because one is studying the biological reaction of one creature with another. The phenomenon are simply being viewed at different levels and perspectives, and in different limited contexts, and different languages.

The sadhaka considers Tantra a science, albeit, one that operates in a far broader arena than what is usually considered science.

Ekam sad vipra bahudha vadanti.
"Truth is one; the wise speak of it in many ways."
Rigveda

Many philosophies

There is no definitive "Tantric philosophy" per se, except the idea that to practice the techniques of Tantra will lead to liberation. To augment and enrich the practice, there is a variety of attendant philosophies. These philosophies or paradigms should be understood as commentary on individual experience, or revelation based on the practice by those *acharyas* (individual teachers) or groups who wish to illumine the experience for other sadhakas. As such they come to us through the filter of the individual or group's cultural circumstances. Each agama or sutra, or any other such document that claims to illumine Tantra is nothing more than an opinion that can only be evaluated in the light of experience of actual practice.

For instance there are Buddhist Vajrayana Tantras and there are Yoga Tantras. The core practices are basically the same with a few minor alterations. However, the philosophies attendant to each of these systems are sometimes light years apart.

Agehananda Bharati in the **Tantric Tradition** states:

"All Tantric philosophy sets forth the power of a conceptual decision, not withstanding the fact that the execution of ritualistic contemplation is carried out in minute detail," and "Tantra is the psycho-experimental interpretation of non-Tantric lore."

The wise Tantric sadhaka avoids the pitfalls of philosophical debate by going directly to the sources, and interpreting them according to their own experience. In this regard Bharati states,

"I also believe that the doctrinary discrepancies between the various schools of speculative thought are really resolved in Tantric sadhana (practice)."

Tantra is not a religion. However, like anything else, it can be made into a religion, and of course this has been done by a variety of sects who have added their peculiar philosophical base to the practice. That is why there are many disagreements about philosophical issues within the body of classical Tantric literature.

The sadhaka is not concerned with philosophical or religious speculation but only with enlightenment. All textual references, such as the agamas, are mere guidelines to be approved or not approved by the true experience of the practitioner. There are no institution-approved "holy scriptures," because there is and there can be no institution with the authority to declare such.

This perspective is not viewed favorably by some sects which have Tantric techniques as part of their discipline. It is problematic for any group trying to assert some kind of "spiritual" authority because it takes the locus of power away from the group and delivers it to the individual.

Bharati, states

"What distinguishes Tantric from other Hindu and Buddhist teaching is its systematic emphasis on the identity of the absolute (*paramartha*) and the phenomenal (*vyavahara*) world when filtered through the experience of sadhana."

Always, the final arbiter of truth in Tantra is the practitioner themselves:

> *Om aham brahmasmi*
> I am the creator, the beginning
> and end of all things.

The yoga of the many and the one

Though there are as many opinions as there are practitioners, one thing remains more or less the same: the sadhana, the practice. This practice is called yoga. The word yoga means a "technique to link." In this context, linking is to the source of all knowledge and wisdom, which thus liberates the Tantric from avidya (ignorance).

The word Tantra can be of some help in understanding a difficult-to-define discipline. As well as meaning "to weave," the word also means to extend, unfold, to continue knowledge. Tantra is a process. This process evolves out of seeming paradox.

There is one point consistent in both Indian and Tibetan-Buddhist based Tantric teachings. This is that absolute reality is a unity which contains within it all polarities of manifestation. Thus the one is many and the many are one. Polarity or duality is considered *maya* (illusion), or to put it another way, the one seen as many. (*Sarvamomkara eva* - all is verily the om). Thus the phenomenal world as we know it, to the Tantric is really one substance appearing as many, or, many substances appearing as one, depending on which view of the paradox you take.

In the *Brihadaranyaka Upanishad* a student asks a teacher "How many gods are there?" The teacher answers "Three thousand and three." The student curiously asks again "How many gods are there?" The teacher replied "thirty three." The student again and again asks the teacher how many gods there are and each time the teacher answers with a diminished number until they get to one. The teacher then explains to the student that they are all manifestations of the one. They are one and the same.

Each bit of creation is considered maya, thus all manifest objects are illusions in as much as they are not perceived as manifesting unity, the reality of being one. Instead they show forth the reality of being many.

Although it is illusion, maya is just as real as the oneness it resides in. One way to understand this is to consider the white light that enters a prism and becomes a rainbow of different colors. The light that appeared to be one color becomes many colors when it goes through the prism. It is exactly the same ray of light, but it has been transformed. You cannot look at the light on one side of the triangular prism and say that this light is real and the light on the other side is not real.

So, the process of Tantra is to resolve the paradox - to understand the nature of diversity, polarity and oneness and the play of these energies - and thus, the nature of the universe.

अं

Savam khalvidam brahma
All this universe is indeed the supreme reality.

Tat twam asi
You are that

Both of these mantras represent the simultaneous meditation on the transcendent and the imminent.

All types of yoga strive for an understanding of the play of diversity, polarity and oneness. This is achieved by the study and practice of balance, at every level of being, with the dynamic of polarity the key focus.

The word *hatha* means sun and moon, and denotes the purpose of hatha yoga, which is to unite or yoke (yoga) the sun and moon together. Sun and moon are male and female, so hatha yoga also means to unite the polarities of male and female, Shiva and Shakti, together in maithuna by a series of physical postures and practices. All yoga addresses itself to the union of opposites to achieve balance; Tantra among them in its particular way.

Samatvam yoga uchyate
Equilibrium is called yoga.
Bhagavad Gita

Delineation of sadhana

The classical literature of yoga delineates four types of yoga: *karma, raja, jnana* and *bhakti*. The type of sadhana is prescribed according to which tattwa (element) is dominant in an individual.

Karma yoga - dominant tattwa: fire; for people who tend to be active.

Raja yoga - dominant tattwa: earth; for people who tend to be empirical and prone to scientific and psychological experimentation.

Jnana yoga - dominant tattwa: air; for people who tend to be reflective and focussed on knowledge gathering.

Bhakti yoga - dominant tattwa water; for people who tend to be emotional and focussed on love. Devotion plays a major role.

Another set of personality categories in classical literature bears mentioning: the grouping of personality types according to three *gunas*. The *tamasic* type tends to materialism, the *rajasic* tends to impetuousness and action. The *sattwic* type tends to reason or think.

These classifications are given their due in Tantric literature, but in practice people are not as easily categorized as these structures imply. Each individual is as unique as their fingerprint, everyone having parts of the rational thinker, the devoted lover, the experimenter, and so on. And, at different times of our lives, we have different tendencies: impulsive, or restrained, or active, or passive.

In its particulars, Tantric sadhana varies as much as people do. Each person has a unique key to unlock their gateway to enlightenment, so the practice must address that key. The sadhaka is the template for the practice. At the level of practice, the self and the not-self in their reciprocity comprise the whole universe. They are a unity, and as the self changes, the not-self is changed.

"What is here is there,
what is not here is not there"
Visvasara Tantra

World view

For the Tantric, the whole of creation is practicing Tantra. All is Tantra! Whether any part of it realizes it or not makes no difference - the cosmos is liberating itself by the very process of existence. It is inevitable that every person, being and object in this universe will become enlightened.

The study of the sciences shows what a fantastic, intricate tapestry the universe is.

From a purely physical point of view, we are the material we are made of, plus the sum of the reciprocal relationships between our components. Everything is rooted in reciprocity. The concept of reciprocity has embedded within it the concept of polarity.

Sentient life, composed of matter at one level, looks upon itself, measures and weighs, and seeks to understand the very nature of what it is. A group of elements have combined to form a creature that can ponder that which formed it and thus reflect upon itself. This is indeed what we are, and the continuing unfolding of knowledge, the process of enlightenment, is Tantra at its most basic level.

Without the fundamental polarity of the perception of self and not-self (the process of individuation), the self cannot be informed by the not-self. There can be no recognition, no revelation. Although our embodiment and individuation can be seen as a limitation that separates us from ultimate unity with the universe, our embodiment is also a gift of revelation. It is an invitation to join in the cosmic dance. The energy of this polarity can be used either to promote further individuation, or be used as a stepladder to cosmic unity. It is simply a matter of perspective. Both paths ultimately lead back to the source, as both yogi and non-yogi die, and the vanities of physical life will be dissolved either way.

Tantra Yoga is a microcosmic version of the macrocosmic process. The difference between the microcosm of individual practice and the macrocosm of universal Tantra, is that the sadhaka consciously uses ritual concentration in time and space with the intent to hasten and even make immediate the process of enlightenment for the benefit and pleasure of those who wish it. At the macrocosmic level, the process goes forward of its own accord whether or not all parts are aware of this movement towards enlightenment.

Time and space are relative. Different perceptions of time, space, unity and diversity are matters of perspective, dependent upon where the perceiver's consciousness is located. Is consciousness locked into the ego of a particular person in a particular time and place, or can it function beyond that limitation? In order to be able to integrate consciousness into the larger macrocosmic whole, a dis-integration of those limitations must take place to a certain degree.

Kali ~ solve et coagula

Within the bounds of time and space, what is constant is perpetual cycles of integration and disintegration, *solve et coagula* (dissolve and condense).

Thus, the material universe is represented by the goddess Kali. Beautiful and horrific, comforting and terrifying, mother Kali, like Saturn in western mythology, eats her children, destroying all she gives birth to. All that is created will become uncreated, everything that is born will die.

Kali is time and space, and the interactions and cycles of interplay that mark all existence. She represents "what is," from the human organismal cycle of birth, life, and death to the birth, life and death of solar systems and galaxies. Life and all other processes are Kali. She embodies the process of manifestation in all worlds: the process of creation, preservation and destruction which is also represented by the Vedic trinity Brahma, Vishnu and Shiva. The sense of "I" (aham) and "this" (idam) is dissolved or destroyed by the Shiva aspect of Kali.

Kali's threefold process of creation, preservation and destruction occurs through the operation of polarity, Shiva-Shakti, as they play out their roles (*lila*) in the drama we call the universe.

The *kama-kala* triangle is the *yantra mandala* (lineal figure) for Kali. In Tantra, it represents the operation of polarity and reciprocity, and various triune concepts that arise from the operation of polarity. One point represents Shiva; another point, Shakti. The third point is created by the interaction between them, the process of balance. This apex is the *bindu* point, *moksha*. The downward pointing triangle is a symbol of the yoni, from which all manifestation comes forth. The upward pointing triangle represents the lingam.

The study of the kama-kala triangle and meditation upon Kali are an extremely important part of the practice of Tantra.

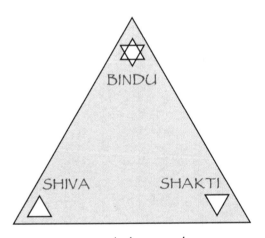

Kama-kala triangle

The kama-kala triangle also represents the three *lokas* (spheres, or planes of existence) called *bhurloka*, *bhuvarloka*, and *svarloka*, which are different dimensions of time and space. Another attribution of the kama-kala triangle is the mental, emotional and physical spheres in which we operate and move.

At yet another level, the kama-kala represents the polarity of our brain function. One point of the triangle represents emotive-emotional right brain function; the other, mental-logical left brain function. Right brain function is attentive to space, the left brain function, to time. The kama-kala is also called the space-time triangle.

The integration, a maithuna, of right and left brain functioning creates bindu, a point of wholeness wherein intuition and intellect inform each other, "in-form" meaning not only to communicate but that they absorb each other. This is also the state in which the individual egoic consciousness can tap into higher levels of consciousness.

For the sadhaka to achieve any level of enlightenment, this maithuna between right and left brain functions must occur. The polarity pairs for this same process are also spoken of as *ida* and *pingala*; *ajna* and *chandra* chakras; *muladhara* and *sahasrara* chakras; and of course, male and female.

In Tantric sadhana, the union of polar opposites is achieved in a variety of ways that involves the totality of our human nature. The intent is to unite our mental, emotional and physical selves in such a way that we can directly connect with the greater universe, and perceive manifestation's unity in diversity.

Ego, samskaras and karma

Within the human subtle bodies are chakras that hold, like knots, various *samskaras*. Samskaras are energy trajectories or karmic trends set in motion in the past that keep us bound to the vagaries of maya, illusion. These patterns and energy flows are held in place by the ideas and attitudes born of our *karma*, our limited perceptions.

To clear the chakras and redirect the energies towards our speedier enlightenment requires disengaging from preconceived notions, feelings, and habits we carry from prior incarnations and our present enculturation - in other words, disengaging from our karma.

The ego is the seat of samskaras, so it is of prime importance for the sadhaka to gain mastery of the ego, rather than being its slave, which seems to be the "normal" human condition. The ego is nothing but part of the illusion matrix, a child of maya, and as such, is heavily invested in maintaining the illusion. The ego seeks to maintain and reproduce itself; and in reproducing it, strengthens the force field of the illusion.

The person who only defines them self according to the limitations of the karma and historical and cultural context of their present life is a slave to their own ego and to maya. They will be run by their samskaras until they finally learn to balance them and hold the reins of karma in their own hands, however many incarnations that may take.

The Tantric, however, is not deluded into thinking that humans can function without ego. Without the play of polarity in time and space, the oneness of the universe cannot be realized. The universe is like a huge game of hide and seek. In order for the play to proceed, there need to be discreet and diverse individuals. We are given our individuality (self) in order to discover the rest of the universe (not-self), and in so doing, discover our true selves.

The ego/personality and all manifestation are gifts that will guide us to enlightenment, eventually. The purpose of Tantric sadhana is to speed up the learning curve and bypass the slower karmic school of hard knocks as much as possible. The Tantric seeks to avoid pain and maximize delight.

Personality takes on a new meaning. The sadhaka realizes that the personality reveals the unique key for each individual to unlock the secrets of the self and the cosmos. By studying and meditating on our own samskaras, we sooner understand how to direct their energies towards our enlightenment. As practice progresses, an intimate relationship forms. Eventually, the initiate of Tantra becomes aware of the limits of even the samskaras as an appropriate learning tool and progresses beyond them to a deeper understanding of life. This is the yoking that is the goal of all yoga.

The true asceticism of yoga and Tantra is realization. It is the ability to not be caught up in the karmic vortexes of the ego. The Tantric grows to viscerally perceive the energy trajectories of their samskaras, in other words, the consequences of their actions, at a much more macroscopic level than the average human being. That perception is extended further in time and space, beyond the limitations of the individual ego and the physical body. So, for instance, the sadhaka can feel the pain that would be caused to others by a particular action at a given time. For the Tantric to participate in that particular action would be like sticking their bare hand into a hot fire.

Conversely, the Tantric can also viscerally feel energy trajectories that lead to joy and ecstasy beyond their own individual selves, and will follow and cultivate them.

An asceticism of attitude

The asceticism of Tantra is not defined by lists of specific activities that are forbidden to the ascetic. The sadhaka is not enjoined, for instance, to "avoid sex or enjoyment because it is an illusion that will bring you down." Instead, the Tantric is told to partake of the joy in sex and all the other fine pleasures of the cosmic illusion, and to appreciate the artistry and wonder of it, knowing that it will take their consciousness higher.

Attitude is everything, and the key to Tantric asceticism. Rulebook types of asceticism essentially condemn and hide from human nature. Tantra accepts life fearlessly and partakes of it fully, knowing:

Sarvam hyetad brahma
All this universe is indeed divine

Sarvam khalvidam brahma
All this universe is indeed the supreme reality

To condemn the nature of the cosmos is foolishness. Sooner or later each person will have to confront all the demons they try to hide from.

There are reasons things are the way they are. To condemn life is to react badly to what we have been given. We may not understand, but to be angry with the cosmos for our own short-sightedness is like sticking your hand into fire and being angry with the fire for burning it. The Tantric seeks to learn quickly from experience, to not put their hand there if they do not want that burning sensation, or wear a fireproof glove, or better yet, the Tantric meditates upon the experience and deepens their understanding of the true nature of fire.

To condemn the process of life is to condemn oneself. It is by the process of life that all unfolds before us in this great wonder to behold.

> *Sarvam eva brahma, namo brahmane*
> All indeed is the divine,
> Reverence to the divine

Condemnation and false asceticism are, from the Tantric view, acts of desperate frustration based on immature understanding of the nature of the cosmos.

Above all, the attitude of the sadhaka towards life is love. Love of life begets openness and curiosity instead of fear, aversion and condemnation. This unconditional love is the basis of Tantra, and the bhakti traditions of yoga, the path of devotion.

> *Om tat sat brahmarpanamastu, om*
> Let there be surrender to the divine,
> the boundless reality

Ego as tool

The average person believes that their ego is who they are, and that is all they have. They are not conscious of their connection to the vastness of the universe and thus to their greater selves. Their definition of themselves and their life purpose is boxed in by their limited perspective.

The personality does not define our whole being. It is a gift to us that gives us focus so that we can plumb the depths of our selves, and explore the cosmos. The Tantric learns to use the ego as a tool to transcend its own limits. Its purpose is to guide us according to our samskaras in the universal Tantra.

Tantric sadhana teaches the practitioner how to wield the ego as a tool. Practices such as pancha makara, bhuta-shuddhi, Shiva Shakti meditation and the study of Kali are all intended to pull the consciousness beyond the ego's limitations.

In order for us to be the masters of our egos, instead of the other way around, it is necessary to weaken the power our ego has over us. Each ego has a trajectory of movement through time and space. Its perceptions are thus limited by the perspective given by its location in time and space. Our liberation from these limitations can only come about when we consciously open up our connection with the universe, and become receptive to the macrocosm. We must unlock the shackles of the personality structure and open up as the yoni opens to receive the lingam.

For most people, the grip of the ego is so tenacious that it has to be threatened with its own demise (in other words, made very aware of physical death) for the person to begin to look beyond themselves and take the leap of consciousness that gets them beyond their ego's limitations.

So, part of Tantric initiation is to confront death. To begin, the Tantric meditates in a graveyard, or cremation ground (*shmashana*). This practice informs us in a very direct way that no matter what our station in life - doctor, lawyer, butcher, baker, or candlestick maker - everyone's end will be the same. All goals in life that the average person so mightily strives for come to an abrupt end and disappear in the mists of time. Each ego is then understood as the most transient of phenomena - one of many skulls in a row.

It is not easy to release ourselves from the narrow passageways of our limited perceptions. However for the Tantric, it is necessary. Tantric practice addresses the powerful fears that bind us into our egos. It is the path of the hero, vira, who relentlessly pursues the light of higher love and knowledge, and struggles with the formidable obstacles, slaying the demons (the fears) that block the way.

Even though the hero does not know exactly what the object of pursuit is, they know, trust and love the scent, and are dedicated to following it into the unknown.

Thus, they become receptive to enlightenment .

The initiate of Tantra pursues enlightenment knowing this:

We don't know the purpose,
but we do know the purpose is
in process as manifestation.
Thus all manifestation is just to the purpose.

Just to the Purpose - ©1996 Phillip & Leigh Hurley

Sexual Morality & Tantra

Morality is generally defined as the principle or standard of right conduct. In our culture, the term is most frequently heard in regard to sexual issues.

A standard of right conduct has at its core the generally accepted principles of right and wrong behavior which are the moral code of a particular community or society. Those who conform to their society's standards are labeled moral or right. Any act not in consonance with the accepted standards of proper sexual behavior as defined by the community is subject to the disapproval of that community.

Those who deviate from their society's standards are considered lewd, licentious, obscene, depraved, wicked, dissolute and profligate.

The eternal problem with this definition of morality is that the concept of right conduct is quite arbitrary.

Nonetheless, many people believe that there exist somewhere inherent universal standards of good and evil. The Tantric understands that there is no such thing.

At the roots of the word "adultery" is the idea of mixing different kinds of things together, i.e., spinning wool together with linen, mating a white cow with a black bull. In certain ancient tribal patriarchal cultures which gave rise to Judaism, Christianity and Islam, the concept was applied to women as well as livestock. At one time the same term meant "to marry into another tribe." It evolved to have connotations of "impurity" and be associated with extramarital sex.

In some cultures it was (and still is in some places) considered appropriate to stone to death people who had sexual congress outside of marriage. This reaction was believed to be the correct response based on community standards of right and wrong.

It should be obvious to us today that to stone people to death simply because they had a sexual interlude is a bit over the top to say the least. In this case, what was considered at one time an appropriate community response, is now considered a criminal act in any civilized country.

It is painfully apparent that community standards of behavior can be dysfunctional, criminal and are often not as well thought out as the average person supposes them to be. They need to be constantly questioned, assessed, and revised.

For the Tantric, community morals have their place for those who need them. They provide a framework for action and thought that is intended to be protective and nurturing of the purposes of the community.

This is all well and good for the average person. Most people need some sort of moral-ethical framework to learn how to relate to others without destroying their own lives and the lives of those around them. However, when it comes to ethical questions of what is right or what is wrong morally, there are no simple answers. The whole concept of right and wrong breaks down in the avalanche of life. Morals must be constantly examined and changed to suit the needs of their historical context.

What does Tantra say about right conduct? In the *Guhyasam-aja Tantra*, Buddha reveals the strange truth that

"The conduct of the passions and attachments (ragacarya) is the same as the conduct of a bodhisattva (bodhisattvacarya)."

Thus what is considered good (moral) is the same as what is considered evil (immoral).

This text also states that perfection can be gained by satisfying all one's desires, sensuality is permitted and the Tantric can commit adultery.

The Tantric perspective of what is considered right and wrong moral conduct is also discussed by Agehananda Bharati, in *The Tantric Tradition:*

"There is a passage in the **Brhadaranyaka Upanishad** which tells how a man should court and consummate a woman - and here there is no reference to whether they are married or not; orthodox pandits aver that it refers to the married man courting his own spouse; but even if this does not follow from the text itself, the vast majority of Sruti or canonical texts presuppose marriage to consummation.

To this the Tantric would answer that the Tantric consecration of a Shakti is of higher order than a marriage ceremony in the Vedic tradition - the fact that it is not accepted by a society ruled by self-styled legislators in matters of moral right and wrong does not concern them."

Not only is conventional morality of no consequence to the Tantric, but what is considered to be immoral is praised, as in the Chinese Tantric legend of the woman from Yen-Chu who gave herself unreservedly to every man she could. After her death, as the legend goes, it was discovered that she was a bodhisattva, whose bones were linked by golden chains, a sign of divinity.

It is a good exercise to contrast this vision with the contemporary view that such a woman by her actions would be considered lewd, lascivious, cheap, and/or mentally deranged, in other words, contemptible instead of worthy of respect. Unfortunately, most people today, with their limited understanding of life, would be hard put to appreciate the beauty and insight of this legend.

Pancha makara, morality and ritual sex

The centerpiece of Tantra is, of course, the chakra puja, pancha makara, which is the ultimate in social sexuality. Here copulation is performed by a selected Shiva and Shakti, or by the group of wor-shippers as a whole with partners. The classical Tantric agamas are laden with expositions of sexual and sensual ritual to which there is nothing comparable elsewhere in the spiritual literature of the world.

Most of the existing literature about Tantric ritual, both agamas and commentary, is written from the perspective of the male sad-haka; and, in the context of a larger culture in which women had very few rights. Some of the most difficult parts of this literature for people to understand are discussions of what sort of women are most suited to participate in the chakra circles, that is, to be channels for Shakti.

Francis King in *Tantra: the Way of Action* has this to say:

"Thus the priestess will perhaps be of a higher caste than the priest, or of a much lower caste, or the wife of another man and thus an adulteress, or even related to the priest in some forbidden degree–perhaps his sister. Such incom-patibility is regarded as so much increasing the efficacy of the ritual copulation that the least favorable combination of priest and priestess is regarded as one in which they are legally married to one another."

"As if to emphasize that it is the goddess who is adored, the woman in whom she is incarnated is sometimes of a type regarded as 'worthless' according to the conventional stan-dards of Indian society. For example she will be a member of an untouchable caste, a prostitute, a dancing girl, or even, according to Tantric legend, a she-demon."

Mircea Eliade in *Yoga, Immortality and Freedom* states, "The more depraved and debauched the woman, the more fit she is for the rite."

Frequently the dombi (washerwoman), or courtesan are mentioned in Tantric writings as the women most like the goddess and capable of being a priestess in the chakra circle. Eliade further states,

"...for only the 'washerwoman' was free from every qualification and attribute, social, religious, ethical, etc."

It can't be said enough that this literature is male centric. Part of the reason for advising that "lowly" women are preferred has to do with the effect on the male sadhaka. He must relate to the consort as goddess in spite of the intense taboos of caste, race and other social strictures. It is a ring-pass-not: the aspirant who cannot pass through and leave behind those taboos is not yet able to perceive, worship and experience the deity, he is too blinded by his samskaras.

Eliade further states,

"It is the symbolism of the 'washerwoman' and the 'courtesan' that is of chief significance, and we must reckon with the fact that, in accordance with the Tantric doctrines of the identity of opposites, the 'noblest and most precious' is hidden precisely in the 'basest and most common.' "

The alchemists of western tradition referred to exactly the same thing when they stated that the *materia prima*, (the Philosopher's Stone, the fundamental basis of all matter), "...was present everywhere and under the basest form." What is considered low or base by conventional wisdom is seen by enlightened wisdom as a key to liberation. This is a theme that runs through many spiritual disciplines.

Shiva - Shakti

In discussing the vital role of the worship of Shiva-Shakti in Tantric tradition, Vivian Worthington in *History of Yoga* states,

"By intense love and worship of the consort - husband, wife or lover - one's own potentiality is enhanced."

The term consort refers to both male and female aspirants. Although Shaktism has been useful in presenting the absolute importance of the role of women in one sense (it is centered on a female archetype/goddess), Shaktism has created much confusion among scholars and would be practitioners today.

Most of the surviving classical literature has been that of Shakti-oriented sects, originally meant for the male worship of Shakti. Shakti literature naturally extols the virtues of Shakti to an extreme as it was meant for a male audience. This is good in that it does show that women were honored and their role in Tantra was vitally important. But, so much confusion and misunderstanding has resulted from this bias that some elucidation is necessary.

It should never be forgotten that Tantra is based upon the coming together of polar opposites. Thus, female practitioners of Tantra devote themselves to Shiva as the key to enlightenment, while male practitioners are devoted to Shakti as the key to enlightenment.

Tantra is not a fertility cult

There is also confusion about the origins and reason-for-being of Tantric sadhana. Some scholars have stated that Tantra is a fertility cult. There could be nothing further from the truth. If, indeed, Tantra was a fertility cult, the literature would be overflowing with mention of pregnancy, and children. As a matter of fact, the retention of semen by the male sadhaka is mentioned in most Tantric treatises as of prime importance.

Even this is popularly misunderstood. It is not that male ejaculation in itself is in any way considered a hindrance to spiritual development. The major purpose of retaining semen is that lengthening the time of ritual intercourse develops not only a greater amount of ecstasy and pleasure among the participants, it also brings kundalini energy into play in ways that do not occur in common sexual activity. And, as should be apparent to all, retention of semen prevents pregnancy, which allows the sadhakas to have control over whether or not they choose to procreate. Having children is probably the heaviest karma people are subject to, so, for both sexes, such control in itself is a major liberation.

There is absolutely no mention of fertility as the goal of Tantra in any of the existing literature. What is in the literature, however, is that the discipline is strictly polarity based, with an emphasis on sensuality and sexuality directed toward the liberation of the participants from *avidya* (ignorance). *Bhoga* (enjoyment) and liberation are the same. Sexuality and sensuality are there to be enjoyed and to be enjoyed with anyone who wishes to participate. There are no moral or caste codes.

This is a shocking realization for most Westerners and East Indians alike.

Tantra has never been well accepted in India. As a matter of fact Bharati in **The Tantric Tradition** states

"Following my own caveat, to distinguish carefully between the 'is' and the 'ought', I would say that Tantrism as a system of practice, as well as a method of thought, as an ideology, has little or no chance in India, but that it ought to be given a chance'.

Even on its home ground, the discipline is reviled by orthodox Vedic Hindus.

Adultery vs. conjugal slavery

Tantric apologists have tried to place Tantric sex as only consummated in the context of marriage, but this is at best a pathetic attempt to gloss over the real nature of Tantra.

One of the most frequent arguments used by the apologists is that the agamas were really of a "twilight language," language that does not mean what it seems to mean on the surface. Indeed twilight language is used by the Tantric, but still, one has to ask why Tantrics would choose to aggravate the general populace with a twilight language that disposes of all conventional moral practices and is guaranteed to offend.

Tantrics not only mean what they say - they also mean more than they say. When a Tantric says, "One can commit adultery," they mean it literally, but they also are saying, in real twilight language, that no one person owns another person's body. This statement is the end of conjugal slavery and threatens whole economic and social systems based upon trade and barter with sex and children as the currency.

At the deepest level, the sadhaka understands that contracts of ownership such as marriage are based on fear of loss. They are powerful attachments that exact a heavy karmic price on those that create and enter into the contractual restrictions. The heavy karmic price is attachment to the object owned to such a degree that it is considered correct to punish the person who breaks that contract. From the Tantric perspective, this attitude is the depths of depravity. To punish someone who does not want to be owned by you anymore is to truly be without inner peace.

Slavery of any kind is not tolerated by the Tantric.

Treading upon the guru

The Tantrics say:

> He who places his foot upon the head of his guru is
> liberated and never reborn.
>
> **Hymn to Kali** (*Karpuradi Stotra*)

Most scholars and Tantric apologists have very little idea of how to handle this phrase. This is due to a lack of good scholarship, but also a lack of understanding of the underlying principles of Tantra, which can only truly be understood by a practitioner.

Guru is the planet which is called Jupiter in western astrology. In Hindu astrology, guru rules traditional religious and philosophical beliefs, as well as lawyers, judges and children. In true understanding of the twilight language, to put your foot on the guru's head means to overcome the restrictions of traditional beliefs, and thus grow into a greater understanding.

It also means to unfetter oneself from the karmic bondage of uncontrolled sexual energy, which materializes downward through our bodies manifesting in procreation of ourselves, having children. The Tantric regards having children as a learning process, not for the children so much as for the parents. Parenthood is an exoteric meditation upon our creative abilities as Shiva and Shakti.

To understand creation and the powers of creation within us as Brahma, some people need to recreate the processes they themselves have been through. It is a path of enlightenment with many shocking surprises. For parents who consider themselves in control of their children and expect that their children will be little models of themselves, there is always a distinct and rude awakening. For those who lack basic traits of responsibility, having children gives an opportunity to learn self-discipline and focus.

The Tantric would say that children are the greatest of gurus, and for the average person, a helpful goad to progress on the path to understanding and wisdom.

The Tantric understands that mother nature's trick of sexual desire and orgasmic pleasure to make humankind want to procreate can be turned back on itself and used to rend the veil of Maya and illusion that she creates. Instead of materializing sexual energies in a downward pattern, that is, having children, the Tantric channels the energies up the spine and consecrates the sexual act to enlightenment.

This is the great wisdom of Tantra.

To avoid being fodder for the machinations of maya, and our own karmic patterns, the sadhaka must turn their back on conventional morality, beliefs and rules of conduct. In any given situation, the Tantric always looks behind the curtain to see who really is the Wizard of Oz pulling the control levers, and why they do what they do.

Contempt for the authority of conventional morality is perceived as the height of blasphemy and egotism by most people.

How dare any mere mortal even contemplate rending the veil of the shared illusion by an act of carnal fornication?

Why do Tantrics choose such methods?

Mother nature

To the Tantric, mother nature is only one of the macrocosms of which we are a microcosm; and she is still a child, an evolving being in a learning process. Her karma is to continue to grow into cosmic adulthood, just as we as individual human beings do. Her most powerful tool (or favorite toy, if you will), is the sexual sensual process wherein she moves creatures to reproduce. She has the power to wield this tool, but she does not fully comprehend the magic and full potential of all that she herself is. Like us, she is looking for her ultimate source and reason for being. She is as much a victim of her own karma as we are victims of ours, in the daily process of living and being.

From the Tantric perspective, it is a mistake for humans to frame their ethics and morality within the limits of mother nature's yet evolving self.

The purpose of the cosmos is still in process. It is not a completed project. To the Tantric, the world was not created in seven days for the benefit of humans, with nothing left to be done but "be fruitful and multiply." It is ever expanding and evolving in complexity. Hidden all around us in plain sight are the seeds of transmutation and transformation in all the world and its creatures - just as they are within us.

Humankind and all other creatures with self reflective awareness are the result of the awakening of macrocosmic kundalini and its actions. We are mother nature and her fate hangs on what we do. We are aware mother earth, we are aware cosmos, looking upon ourselves and what we are made of. We are not just ourselves within a framework of nature - we are mother nature, and her awareness is our awareness.

As we change, mother nature, all the world around us, is changed. And just as we are confused by change, mother nature also is confused by change even when wrought by her own hand. She is slow and cumbersome. Her liberation or enlightenment proceeds from her conscious awareness of herself and her processes.

Our conscious awareness is part of her conscious awareness. This conscious awareness or feedback mechanism is inherent in all her processes and karma, as it is in ours. Mother nature or matter "saves" (enlightens) itself, as we do, through the operation of polarity. Without the play of polarity, some consciousness of self and other, there is no life, no feedback.

At all levels, mother nature is in constant maithuna with all that she is. How does this occur?

It is by the interactions of the process of polarity that all manifestation grows to know itself, that manifestation grows in gnosis.

Lucifer - nature enlightened

In western traditions, the interaction of form and subsequent gnosis is reflected in the mythology of Lucifer. Lucifer is Satan, but not Satan as popularly interpreted. Satan, who is also the planet Saturn and represents all manifestation, just as Kali does, is illusion or maya, but the illusion has an enlightening component. Lucifer means light bearer. Light can only be perceived when there is non-lightness (darkness) present to some degree. And, only through polarity can oneness be perceived.

In the mythology of Satan, the seed for the evolution of the soul, enlightenment, is found in matter and its polarity interactions. Saturn (*Sani* in Sanskrit) rules matter and its consequent karma, the action of polarity. The seat of Saturn/Lucifer/Kali is the *muladhara* chakra, the very heart of matter. The muladhara is the lowest chakra on the spine, and it is no mistake that kundalini energy, the key to enlightenment, is based there.

The interactions of matter and our awareness of these interactions are the key to Tantra and spiritual realization.

James Braha in his *Ancient Hindu Astrology for the Modern Western Astrologer* has this to say about Saturn:

"Although Saturn's very nature is to restrict, deny, and destroy, it also, as one of the two outer planets in Hindu astrology, is capable of bestowing the greatest evolutionary qualities a person may possess."

"This may be related to the fact that the wisdom indicated by Saturn has been gained by experience rather than by philosophy or intelligence, as is the case with Jupiter, the other spiritual planet".

Both philosophy and intelligence are mainly left brain operations. Actual experience is a mostly right brain activity and builds intuition.

The gnosis given by Saturn is about deep contemplation upon form. It is the knowledge of a good carpenter who by experience knows their materials and can immediately feel exactly what can be done with any given piece of wood.

In Hindu astrology Saturn not only rules wisdom gained by personal experience, but also spirituality, non-attachment, asceticism, ascetics, monks, hermits. It is directly related to Shiva the destroyer, and Marah or Maya, the great Shakti, the mother of all form.

This dual symbolism shows the inherent polarity makeup of all organization, structure and form, and all that proceeds from the interactions of those polarities.

Together, Shiva and Shakti are the fundamental polarity pair, and together as a pair in their wholeness they are Kali the great goddess, mother nature. Kali is every process of the cosmos; and every process of the cosmos is a polarity process.

Mother nature eats her children

In mythology Kali eats her children, meaning that what is born into existence must also die in the cycle of nature. Thus to a Tantric, to give birth is also to sacrifice the child you give birth to. Every child, every human dies, thus every birth is a sacrifice to the goddess Kali. From a Tantric point of view, child sacrifice, which to most moderns is a repugnant idea, is actually occurring constantly on a daily basis within our very own midst.

The purpose of this child sacrifice is to add to the conscious awareness of nature, to add another facet to the prism of creation. Kali, mother nature, thinks she can redeem herself in this manner.

She is in just as much of a frenzy to understand what she is about as we are. She speculates, mentates, and experiments genetically. She creates more and more mentators and speculators and experimenters to find the cause of her own being and her true nature.

In western traditions, for instance, the ancient Hebrews sacrificed children by inserting them into the cornerstones of buildings as a direct offering. Many other cultures had similar pasts in which sacrifice was as direct and to the point. The story of Abraham, the father willing to sacrifice his son is a direct tale of the sacrifice required by the nature god YHVH.

And, from the Hebrew tradition sprang the mythology of the virgin birth and the Christ figure.

The Tantric sees in this story mother nature/Mary/Marah's attempt to bring forth the flower of spiritual insight into matter. It is the rising kundalini in Marah's soul.

Mary, as legend has it, gives birth to a spiritual teacher who upon disseminating his insight is promptly dispatched in a most cruel fashion. He is sacrificed, and through his sacrifice all others, according to the legend, can be saved. Mary/Marah/mother nature weeps for her son, and becomes aware of her sacrificial nature - but, she also knows that the sacrifice will bring light to the world.

For the Tantric, this story is the tale of every birth and death, for every human brings light to the world; and they sacrifice their lives to do so because every birth of an individual requires the death of that individual. This is why the sadhaka prepares for initiation by meditating in a shmashana (graveyard, or cremation grounds). "All humans end here" is the lesson, unless the life force (kundalini energy) is redirected up the spine. Form begets more form and so on, in rounds and rounds of samskara... or, that energy can be turned back on itself.

The Christ legend has many facets, but one lesson to cull from it is that if you are going to have children and sacrifice them in the fires of life, at least raise them to move us forward and through the veil of illusion. It is ignorant from the Tantric perspective, to have children simply to satisfy your petty ego and play god by creating and manipulating what you may think is a miniature version of yourself.

Tantrics view child bearing as a awesome undertaking because the birthing of a child is also a death sentence for that child. Their vision of children is quite different from that of the everyday masses. They do not ignore the gruesome realities of Kali. They have the final understanding of the Mary of legend who views her dead son sacrificed. The beauty of the story however is in the quality of the life force that she brought into the world.

Birth is a rite of sacrifice to the goddess of nature, to the Tantric, and no matter how much one tries to hide from the reality of all that the sacrifice entails, it is always there. It is the dark side of Mary/Marah/Kali, it is her sorrow we see in the Pieta, and it is a message to the world to contemplate the world vision. She is saying, "Where do we go with all this?"

The heart of the legend is that by individual human sacrifice, the jewel of wisdom can be found beyond the limitations of Kali/mother nature, but only by turning one's back on convention and norms. It was the Nazarene's contempt of norms that got him crucified.

Defying karmic gravity

There are two different evolutionary paths, expressed astrologically in the concept of the juxtaposition of Jupiter and Saturn as a polarity pair. Here Jupiter represents norms, laws, and conventions, while Saturn represents the shunning and violation of them through asceticism.

What type of asceticism? Tantric asceticism is not asceticism as popularly imagined, in which one simply exchanges the conventions and rules of the masses for the conventions and rules of some religious institution.

It is an asceticism of attitude and understanding. The sadhaka, always fearless and questioning, looks beyond maya, the illusion. We draw back the veil of maya, just as Dorothy's courage and questioning prompted her to draw back the curtain on the Wizard of Oz, who was, after all, no real wizard, but just a simple mortal who needed Dorothy's help to get back home himself.

Here the Tantric slyly insinuates that "God needs help and we are here to do the job." It is a waste of one's life energy here, and everybody else's too to never expose and look beyond the god of "be fruitful and multiply," and "follow my commandments and I will reward you. If you don't, I will punish you," (the Wizard's tactics).

Most conventional wisdom and most of the world's major religious traditions say that sex is for procreation, not for spiritual enlightenment. This has created a child-bearing cult of great magnitude. It is so ingrained in us that people very rarely ask *why* they should have children. They consider it a duty. This is the work of maya, the illusion.

The sadhaka examines the relationship between form and energy, and thus our lives, on both a mundane and cosmic scale. This reconsideration, contemplation, and meditation increases our perceptual abilities beyond the norm. It is far-sighted, unconventional wisdom.

Many religious traditions teach that sexuality and sensuality (and thus, mother nature) are forces too powerful for humans to wield responsibly. There are many taboos in this regard, which are quite embedded in most of the world's cultures, no matter how "modern." As a result, the average person is quite inhibited about their sexuality and sensuality, and this condition keeps them ignorant and without control of a huge portion of themselves. This ignorance and inhibition allows the powerful energies of human life force to be channeled into tight social and religious structures... for the perpetuation of those institutions and the status quo, frequently at the individual's expense - again, human sacrifice. From the perspective of these structures, sensuality and sexuality must be channeled to create more church members, more consumers, more workers, more taxpayers, more soldiers and so on.

Conventional wisdom supports a fertility-focused bio-cult centered on raising children, giving blind obeisance to mother nature's compulsion for each species to try to multiply itself and engage in evolution by trial and error.

In contrast, the point of Tantra is intentional evolution, and the energies of sexuality and sensuality are focussed and consciously used to move quickly in that spiritual evolution.

There is no mention of childbearing as a spiritual duty in any of the existing literature in classical yoga. On the contrary, the literature of yoga generally advises disengagement from such mundane occupations.

The intent of Tantra is moksha, liberation from the mundane, by the redirection and focus of kundalini energy. This does not mean that either having children or not having children is in itself viewed as good or bad. It is simply that the sadhaka understands more of the karma involved with either choice, and consciously and responsibly makes that choice for them self.

If a person is unfocussed and allows their kundalini energy to create and manifest in a downward arc, which is where the "gravity" of natural processes (mother nature) will tend to take it, then children will likely be the result. If one wishes to refine and direct kundalini, this energy is focussed upward and beyond the "gravity" of mother nature, and speeds both our enlightenment and hers. In both cases, the starting point is the same: the passion of polarity. However, what we do with it and where we go with it, is quite different.

Conventional morality is inherently tied up with religious paradigms that have child bearing as their centerpiece. This puts it in direct conflict with Tantra. Tantrics do not deny the validity of the joys of certain pursuits. If you enjoy bearing and rearing children, then that is good. If one has children because conventional wisdom expects it, or to create slaves that will, for instance, take care of you in your old age, that is not so good. Tantra is definitely not a mother and apple pie tradition. It is the tradition of the whore and libertine by puritan moralist standards.

Tantrism is a powerfully liberating discipline for woman. The bondage of women to the roles of child bearer and rearer without choice is repugnant to the Tantric. It is only in recent times, through much effort that women have begun to assert themselves and take on other roles. Even so, when a woman today says "I do not want children" there is still frequently a sense of unease amongst the hearers.

The moral rebel as hero

Most Christian sects support and sanctify a cult of fertility, and thus child rearing, as the apex of their tradition, but oddly enough their source traditions and teachings warn against being caught up this way in the status quo, unless one absolutely has to and can't control their sexual desire. In *1 Corinthians 7:1-2* Paul states,

"Now for the matters you wrote about: It is good for a man not to marry. But since there is so much immorality, each man should have his own wife, and each woman her own husband."

In *1 Corinthians 7:8-9*

"Now to the unmarried and the widows I say: It is good for them to stay unmarried, as I am. But if they cannot control themselves, they should marry, for it is better to marry than to burn with passion."

Paul's statement is in the context of "no marriage means no children." Thus one of the most prominent leaders of the Christian church in its formative stages relegates the role of marriage and producing children, to the category of something to be avoided if possible.

Although the context is quite different, and the reasoning at odds with Tantra on some points, one can see in Paul's contemplations a shift from the fertility/bio-cult paradigm toward a model based on the redirection of life energies to another goal. Paul's position is a result of his direct modeling upon the life of the Nazarene, who did not marry and spent his life questioning the conventional wisdom of the times. Such questioning is the birth of all new paradigms. In *Luke 14:26* the Nazarene states:

"If any man come to me, and hate not his father, and mother, and wife, and children, and brethren, and sister, yea, and his own life also, he cannot be my disciple."

Although it sounds harsh, the meaning of this exhortation is that if you are not dissatisfied with conventional wisdom and ways, and you do not understand them to be lacking, then you will not be able to proceed spiritually.

In similar harsh tones in **Matthew 10:34-38,** the Nazarene states

"Do not suppose that I have come to bring peace to the earth. I did not come to bring peace, but a sword. For I have come to turn a man against his father, a daughter against her mother, a daughter-in-law against her mother-in-law, a man's enemies will be the members of his own household."

This phrase expresses a powerful understanding of what the new paradigm will do to the structure of the society and culture.

Socrates of Athens and his rule to question the society you live in and the world around you rings a similar note. Socrates stated "The unexamined life is not worth living for the Human being." He was a critic of conventional wisdom who constantly questioned societal principle, people's assumptions and the traditions of Athenian life. He also saw the need to be critical of both those around us and of ourselves; and he too, had a new concept of what a human being is and could be.

Both Socrates and the Nazarene, were tried at the hands of conventional wisdom and sentenced to their deaths for their audacity to question conventional wisdom. Just as a good Tantric would, both Socrates and the Nazarene mocked their judges: the Nazarene mocked through his silence to Pilate's accusations, and Socrates through his absolutely abusive verbal detraction of his executioners. Both were recognized as heroes (*vira*) after they were sacrificed.

They were considered enemies of conventional morality and wisdom, that is, the state and its institutions. Socrates was sentenced to death for "undermining the state religion and corrupting the youth" and the Nazarene on a multitude of similar charges, as well as petty criminal charges, probably including thrashing the money changers with a whip; and overturning tables and disrupting business at the Temple.

In the words of the Nazarene, the possible results of replacing conventional wisdom with a different order of things are *Luke 21:16*

"You shall be betrayed both by parents, and brethren and kinfolks, and friends; and some of you shall they cause to be put to death."

These stories from western tradition speak of the same aspect of evolving human consciousness that Tantrics refer to when they say that only the vira (hero) is fit for the path of Tantric discipline. Fear causes people to be enslaved to maya, the illusion, and holds back the evolution of human and planetary consciousness, both at the microcosmic and macrocosmic levels. Very simply put, no guts, no glory.

अं

The ancient Poets animated all sensible objects with Gods or Geniuses,
calling them by the names and adorning them with the properties of
woods, rivers, mountains, lakes, cities, nations,
and whatever their enlarged & numerous senses could perceive.

And particularly they studied the genius of each city & country,
placing it under its mental deity;
Till a system was formed, which some took advantage of & enslav'd
the vulgar by attempting to realize or abstract
the mental deities from their objects: thus began Priesthood;
Choosing forms of worship from poetic tales.

And at length they pronounc'd that
the Gods had order'd such things.

Thus men forgot that
All deities reside in the human breast.

from The Marriage of Heaven and Hell
- William Blake

Initiation into Vama Marga, the Left-Hand Path

A vamacharin is someone who is initiated into the vama marga, the so-called left-hand path of Tantra. This initiation can take many forms.

The first step for the aspirant on the path of vama marga is to dedicate them self and their life to discovery, enlightenment.

This act of dedication brings a knowledge, a wisdom and, a power that is beyond the normal range of human experience. This knowledge, wisdom and power is called *siddhi* in yoga tradition. Siddhi begins to occur at the time of dedication, because the very act of dedication begins the removal of obstacles to enlightenment. This is because the whole of our being becomes fully engaged with our quest for discovery.

It is not possible to dedicate oneself to discovery with a closed mind and the presumption that one already has all the answers. All former ideas and beliefs must be sacrificed in the fires before entering the temple for initiation, which is the act of dedication. If former ideas and beliefs are consonant with the new discoveries after initiation, they will resurface in new form. So, ultimately nothing really is lost, but the would-be initiate must divest them self of former patterns, dissolving them into their primordial elements and restructuring them. They must become a blank slate and begin anew without the encumbrances of energy patterns that do not serve spiritual freedom.

It is like composting. Old forms decay to form rich earth that will support new and fresh life forms. It is the alchemical *solve et coagula* (dissolve and reform), represented by the phoenix rising from the ashes, born anew.

Samskaric tendencies from the past are the basis for the average person's daily life - their hopes, fears, wishes and actions. The act of dedication begins to dissolve the energy patterns that we run in our everyday lives and frees that energy to create new forms.

On the surface, the act of dedication seems very simple, but it is not so easy. We all have identity patterns based on our past achievements and actions, but very few people identify themselves by what they are to become.

The first type of identity is limited because it is based on the past, which cannot be changed. The second is boundless, because it is based on the future, where you are going and what you are to become. And, for those who dedicate themselves, every movement and all possibilities lead to enlightenment.

The ritual of initiation

The aspirant to vama marga leaves all outer trappings (clothes, jewelry, etc.) behind before entering the temple or circle for the dedication ceremony. This ritual gesture shows the aspirant's sincerity in divesting and disengaging from the energy patterns of the samskaras that have kept them from enlightenment. Totally naked, the aspirant enters the temple or circle, ready for their new adventure as vira or hero.

To open the temple, a bell is rung three times to gather the spirits such as the *devas* and *apsaras* to witness this event. These "spirits" are conscious embodiments of particular cosmic and life processes and energies. Upon being made aware that the person before them is to become an initiate, their relationship to the aspirant changes and they are eager to assist the aspirant's journey.

As the bell is rung, the opening of the temple is performed by one of the shaktis within the center of the chakra, or circle of initiates. The aspirant is led to the outer rim of the circle to observe Shakti seated and spreading her legs so that her yoni is visible to all. Once Shakti has performed the opening asana, she retires to the circle and joins the others. The initiate is led to the center of the chakra and assumes the lotus position facing east or sunrise point for that time of year. There are a variety of mantras that the aspirant then pronounces.

The most important of these are:

Aum aham brahma smi
(I am Brahma-the creator)

Aum aham kali smi
(I am Kali), and

Aum aham shiva smi
(I am Shiva (males)), or
Aum aham Shakti smi-
(I am Shakti (females)).

Thus a new identity is born.

Following these mantras, either Shakti or Shiva is evoked. Males evoke Shakti by reciting, "*Shakti ahum*" (come to me Shakti), females evoke Shiva by reciting, "*Shiva ahum*" (come to me Shiva). From the circle, either Shakti or Shiva will emerge and sit before the aspirant in the Lotus position and wait to perform maha mudra/maithuna with the initiate. Thus Shakti or Shiva comes to aid, consort with, and comfort the aspirant in their journey.

The aspirant at this time performs puja upon Shiva or Shakti by kissing the heart chakra, the yoni or lingam and the feet of the consort. The puja is completed by performing maha mudra/maithuna.

The consort then gives a physical token of initiation to the aspirant, who is now an initiate. This is usually a wand with seven bands to represent the seven planets and the powers they represent, or five bands for the five elements. The token can also be a symbol of Shiva lingam or Shakti yoni, or any other object deemed appropriate.

The bell is rung three times again to end the ceremony.

The ritual of initiation can be much more elaborate, or much simpler depending on circumstances or choice. The exact form of the ritual is not critical. The aspirant should not hesitate to use their own creativity, which is the expression of their own magical self.

The simplest initiation ceremony consists of one person, who, with clear intention, dedicates them self to discovery and enlightenment. No bells and whistles, just you and the cosmos linking through dedication, becoming one, a maithuna. This is probably the most practiced initiation as it is often not easy to find chakra circles.

Shiva Shakti Meditation

Part 1
Contemplation on polarity

Time and space, and thus our consciousness, is defined by the play of the five elements: earth, water, fire, air and akasha; as we perceive that play through our five senses. The universe reveals itself to sentient organisms such as ourselves through sound, sight, touch, taste, and smell.

Each form or objectified piece of existence has a rate of vibration, a frequency that it "tunes" us into when we sense it through our biological receptors. We are informed about the objects in our environment constantly. A wide range of frequencies calls for our attention and creates the general background noise we live in.

We all repress certain signals from the environment and allow others to surface in our consciousness. This is necessary for everyday living, and for us to have a sense of self in a myriad of phenomenon. To let everything in at once would create confusion, like a radio tuned to several stations simultaneously: the sound from it becomes unpleasant and stressful.

All the ambient data we receive is filtered through five of our chakras, then sorted according to our particular samskaras and acted upon or not, depending on our attitude and our general karma. The chakras as they relate to our senses are:

muladhara   - smell
svadhisthana   - taste
manipura   - sight
anahata   - touch
vishuddha   - hearing.

Our samskaras are our karmic tendencies and patterns. They are neither good nor bad in and of themselves. They act as the filters in our chakras, through which some data are allowed to come to consciousness while other data are rerouted and stored at a subconscious level. If too much data from our perceptions of form are routed by our samskaras to the subconscious, the chakras can become blocked. This blockage can manifest as dysfunctional behavior until the energy produced by these forms is brought to the light of day and transmuted.

In meditation, the intent is to tune out the background noise of our daily environment and totally fill our consciousness with a selected vibration, without static.

When we focus on a particular form and lock our attention into it, it is like tuning a radio to a particular station. As in radio, when we tune into a frequency, we become aware of what that frequency has to offer, the music or other program of our choice. Our attention, focus and dedication tunes us into the object of our meditation and we become a receiver of the vibratory rate of the object.

The process is: we perceive the object, which is how we catch the frequency, and then we allow the object to tune us into its particular vibration to the exclusion of all else. Our consciousness takes on the form of the object

Such focus changes our time-space context, just as when we become fully engaged in reading a novel, or in performing some task, we are carried away by the object of our attention. We have moments in which we forget "ourselves" in the context of the world that centers on that object or task, and the sensory input we receive from it.

It is the inherent nature of all form to want to be known and be one with the knower. Con-templation and meditation are a bridge from the perceiver to form. The cosmos presents itself to us as time and space, form and line.

Ideally, in the act of meditation upon form, the Tantric's consciousness is so fully engaged by the form contemplated that they loose all sense of self. The contemplator allows the form to envelope and guide them, and "inform" them ever so gently, and the essence of the form is revealed to them. This evocation of the essence of form by meditation on it is called *samyama* in yoga.

So, the core practice of Tantric meditation is to repetitively focus and lock our attention into a form, most preferably a Shiva or Shakti.

Temple, template, contemplate

The words contemplate, template and temple have a common source. As well as meaning a place delineated for religious or spiritual activities, the word temple refers to a guide device to keep cloth in a loom stretched to its correct width during weaving. One meaning of the word Tantra is to weave.

A template is a form which guides a process. What is con-templated guides and in-forms the consciousness of the meditator.

The sadhana (template, practice) of Tantra, is a technique to perceive, it does not tell us what to perceive. It is a minimal framework to help the sadhaka on their journey of meditation. A ladder can help us ascend to heights, but the ladder itself is not the heights; it is the means for us to proceed towards our goal.

Tantra uses the human form as the template, because it is the thing that we are most intimate with. It is the beginning and end of all things for us as humans. It is the form that defines our existence on this plane, and is our primary perceptual structure for understanding the cosmos.

As members of the human species, we are most immediately and intimately defined by our polar opposite, humans of the opposite sex. As with the electromagnetic forces that hold subatomic polarity pairs in relationship to each other, there is a natural biological force that draws female to male and vice versa.

Leonardo Da Vinci's Vitruvian Man presents
the human body as a microcosm of the universe,
an important Tantric concept.

Any one thing is woven in with every other thing in time and space, thus meditation upon one thing can connect us with everything else in the universe.

"To see a world in a grain of sand,
And a heaven in a wild flower,
Hold infinity in the palm of your hand,
And eternity in an hour."
William Blake

We could, as the poet Blake suggests, meditate upon a grain of sand and await revelation; or we can, as a Tantric prefers, meditate on the form of a nude woman or man.

Meditating upon the naked body of the opposite sex evokes a much stronger response in us. It is a total organismal experience that communicates to us immediately and fully as no grain of sand ever could. Our whole being becomes engaged at many different levels. The energy generated forms an immediate bridge between the sadhaka and the Shiva or Shakti, because of the natural tendencies for opposites to attract and complete the movement of coming together within the kama-kala triangle.

In the process of devoted contemplation, the temple is formed. In Tantra, the template which creates the temple is the physical body of Shiva or Shakti. For the male sadhaka, Shakti is the form that brings revelation; and for the female sadhaka, Shiva is the form that brings revelation. The natural interplay of polarity creates energy, like the powerful attraction between the opposite poles of two magnets. This natural affinity easily engages us, to great benefit.

Fundamental polarity

Any form, from the microcosmic to the macrocosmic, exists only in the context of its reciprocal relationship to everything else in the universe, and most particularly, its polar opposite. Polar opposites are closely defined, readily discernible relationships that have immediate impact upon each other.

For instance, you cannot really define an electron, a negatively charged particle, in and of itself. It only exists because of its relationship to its polar opposite, a proton, a positively charged particle. If you could, for instance, remove all electrons from the universe, everything else would collapse. Everything within this universe is built upon the reciprocal nature of polar opposites. With no electron, there would be no proton; and with no female, there would be no male. This is the nature of time and space, and the pairing of Shiva and Shakti.

The female body can only be understood in the context of relationship to a male form and body, its immediate polar opposite, and vice versa. They are designed for communion with each other.

This is obvious, but what may not be so obvious is that if you took either one of these polarities away, the other would cease to exist. Both forms would be gone. Shiva is defined and kept in existence by Shakti; and Shakti is defined and kept in existence by Shiva.

Shiva/Shakti meditation leads our consciousness to connect with the essential nature of the cosmos. Although the knowledge of and connection with "the beginning and end of all things" is contained within every object and being, the Tantric prefers the human body of the opposite sex as the ultimate form for their meditation. This is a choice based upon an experienced understanding of human nature. It was through such Tantric meditation upon the human form that knowledge of chakras, ayurveda, and other esoteric sciences were revealed and developed.

At its most fundamental, the subject of Tantric meditation is the fabric of time-space: the weave of it and its meaning, the way things are connected.

"What is here is there,
what is not here is not there"
Visvasara Tantra

The kama-kala triangle represents the dynamic of polarity in space and time, the relationship between the knower and the object of contemplation. The relationship between them creates transformation, enlightenment. The subject by contemplating the object discovers the reconciling principle in the process of contemplation.

The words in-form and con-template speak of how the observer is changed by what is observed.

This is the principle of polarity, the nature of relationships and the mystical significance of, for instance, the Trinity in Christian theology. The Holy Spirit in the Trinity is that which in-forms and inspires to deeper understanding.

This process of "inspiration" or taking in, is a communion, a coming together, a union of opposites: the self and the not-self,

Shiva and Shakti. We are led to the discovery of the true nature of time and space through intimacy and inspiration. This process of coming together through contemplation and other practices is "worship" for the Tantric.

So, in pursuit of further enlightenment and self-knowledge, to attempt to penetrate the mysteries of time and space, the Tantric contemplates the communion of opposites. To contemplate our immediate polar opposite, that which truly defines us in our capacity as male or female, leads to a knowledge of the self. We must understand our opposite polarity in order to understand ourselves and why we are. This is meant in the most mundane as well as in the most transcendent sense.

In Vivian Worthington's *A History of Yoga* he states "In these ancient systems, the most basic of human functions were worshipped and placated."

In the excavations at Mohenjo Daro and Harappa can be found traces of the worship of the male principle in the form of the lingam (phallus) and the female principle in the form of the yoni (vulva).

When these two polarities are brought together, right brain and left meld in communion to create a whole, the bindu. The most basic aspects of our nature become the seat of enlightenment and open the most profound avenues of inquiry.

Balancing intellect and intuition

There is great promise in Tantra but only for those who can balance and reconcile left brain intellect with right brain intuition and its language of form. The Tantric always seeks to combine them, to bring the two halves together in a maithuna. Form is intuition, intuition is knowledge, and knowledge is power and liberation. Those who aspire to practice Tantra must understand that the left brain intellect is just half of the picture. Only then are they ready for Shiva/Shakti meditation.

The Tantric considers all bodies of knowledge to be, at one level or another, communion with the "divine", the essence of the cosmos, but any particular body of knowledge has limits. Unlike science, Tantra gives full credentials to intuition as real knowledge.

Science is based solely upon logic, left brain function, and denies the validity of intuitive perceptions in the quest for understanding the nature of the universe. This left brain bias has left us with a cultural deficit that is staggering in its proportions. In this world view, the arts are considered entertainment only, something for our amusement, while the "serious" stuff of life is that which can be calculated and measured.

It is the sad story of a man who once met a very beautiful woman. She made his heart stop and his breath was taken away, and all he knew is that all he wanted to do was experience this woman for the rest of his life in blissful communion. "But alas," he said to himself, "I have no money so I must go out and earn the money and when I have money the woman will desire me and want to marry me and thus my wish will come true." So began his slide down the slippery slope of left brain thinking. He worked very hard, got two jobs and went to school at nights so he could even get a better job and make more money. Of course, work and school took up most of this gentleman's time; so he had hardly any time to spend with this beautiful woman of his dreams. As fate would have it, by the time he felt he was ready for the final play and make this goddess his very own, she was gone. Apparently tired of being lonely, she found a lover who, understanding the meditation of relationships, did not allow Tantra to be overshadowed by intellectual concerns.

For the Tantric, science and intellect are tools that exist to further our enjoyment of life. To take leave of the forms that stir our souls, and to stay in the counting house is counterproductive. When the horse rides us rather than vice versa we have become a slave to what was supposed to serve us, and we lose the object of our intent. We become something we never intended to be.

The Tantric understands that everything is rooted in reciprocity. If you are in a relationship, and your consciousness and attention are elsewhere, that relationship disappears. Your life revolves around and becomes defined by whatever you circle with your mind and are attentive to.

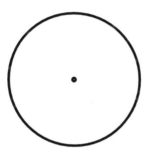

"We dance around in a ring and suppose,
but the Secret sits in the middle and knows."
The Secret Sits - *Robert Frost*

अ

Part 2

Creativity, intellect and intuition

Intuition, art and all science are based on the relationships of things to one another. All movement of energy through time and space is dependent on the action of the reciprocal nature of form. The yin and yang of existence creates all movement and karma.

The art and science of Feng Shui answers the question of what to do with form in time and space. Thus Shiva Shakti meditation is a form of Feng Shui, and a component of Taoist Yoga. The shape or form of one particular thing fits exactly into place among the forms of all other things. The sadhaka contemplates one form, and in understanding it most deeply, all other forms can be understood.

Through the flow of form and line, the cosmos reveals its essence in myriad ways. Geometry is a language. Plato, amongst others, considered geometry sacred. Time and space are forms and lines, all related to each other. The relationships can be perceived by us through numbers or aesthetics, two different ways of cognizing the same phenomenon.

Art: intuition vs. emotion

We intuit form. Intuition is feeling, and feeling is awareness. But, feeling must not be confused with what we call emotion. Emotion is a reaction to feeling developed from samskaras, but emotion is not the feeling itself.

The artist employs both left brain and right brain to produce forms that provoke certain feelings in the observer. To do this, the artist "feels" the object of study by contemplation and meditation. Then the artist develops the concept appropriately for expression in the media employed, which requires some technical left brain competence. The artist must also choose which element or dominant feeling to reproduce. It may be that the artist decides to try to convey the exact nature of what they see, or only reveal to the observer, by art, a portion of that nature according to their individual inspiration, and their own samskaras.

Art can be intended to communicate to others, or as a process of discovery for the artist, or both.

In *Serpent In The Sky*, author John Anthony West states,

"Even today there is a kind of 'art' that is intended to guide the performers along the road to consciousness, though we tend not to think of this as 'art' but rather as exercise or discipline. Into this category of art fall Zen archery and painting, tea-making and the martial arts, and the dances of the Dervishes and of the temple dancers of India and Bali. With the possible exception of Zen painting, these arts are not meant to 'communicate'. Watch a Dervish dance and you get nothing from it. Try to do a Dervish dance and you will be in for a big surprise."

Still, art performed simply for self-realization can have a residual effect on even the most casual observer due to the naturally enlightening nature of form.

Each of us is a template formed by our network of understanding (karma). Our karma literally influences the objects we perceive.

It is problematic to explain the nature of Shiva Shakti meditation and the experiences related to the practice. Our conceptual networks are bound by words and explanations that are useful but woefully limited. It is one thing to be in full awareness with understanding, that is, cosmic consciousness or *satori* (an enlightening experience); but it is quite another thing to convey that experience to someone else. The fullness of the experience has to be reduced to the limits of spoken language to communicate it to others in words. At best, words can only point to it.

Still, there are many different ways to point to experiences with words. One can describe the rising sun at certain times of year in precise astronomical terms with calculations showing the position of the moon and other celestial bodies; or, one can express it poetically as Omar Khayyam did in his **Rubaiyat**:

> "Awake! For morning in the bowl of night
> has flung the stone that puts
> the stars to flight and lo!
> The Hunter of the East has caught
> the Sultans Turret in a Noose of Light."

It is to our great benefit that Omar saw fit to try to engage us as best he could with his experience as there are many scientists with calculators but very few Omars.

Part 3
Traditional puja

The agamas generally speak of two forms of *puja* (an act of devotion): *manasi* puja (mental worship, generally internal), and *bahya* puja (physical worship, external activities).

Puja is most effective if it engages our total emotional, physical and mental capacities.

Bahya puja engages the mind and emotions, and leads the sadhaka swiftly through the maze of competing external phenomenon to focus contemplation upon the *pratima* (object) of worship. *Mantra* focuses the mind. Contemplation of the qualities of either Shiva or Shakti and their purpose for us, engages our emotions. By actively involving us mentally, emotionally and physically, the process of puja connects us to Shiva or Shakti and allows the pratima to be infused with *prana-pratistha*, life principle.

Shiva or Shakti, the deity in human form, can be represented by anything from a live person to a painting, photograph or sculpture. The meditation takes the form of *upasana*, waiting upon, or literally, "sitting near," Shiva or Shakti, and includes activities such as adoration, contemplation, and invocation or evocation using images, emblems or diagrams (geometric figures) which represent Shiva/Shakti.

Emblems of the lingam and yoni are used extensively, and are the centerpiece for most Tantric temples. Diagrams and geometric figures are called yantras or mandalas, and include linear elements within the diagrams which represent certain forces. For instance, a downward pointing triangle represents the yoni/Shakti, and an upward pointing triangle represents the lingam/Shiva.

The *upasaka* (worshipper) places these pratima (person, images, emblems, diagrams) before themselves as a *pratika* (symbol) to perform adoration and puja (worship).

Elements of puja

The external components of puja vary from one tradition to another, however sixteen *upacharas* (ritual elements) are usually the basis of puja. Many of these particular upacharas are used for a number of purposes and can be included or not in ritual puja, depending upon the intention of the worshiper.

Asana, the seating of the image and the upasaka. At its most basic, this consists of choosing the representation of Shiva/Shakti for practice and placing them in an appropriate location. It is also the seat or position the sadhaka will take before the pratima. This is usually *padmasana* (lotus position), but can be any position the worshipper chooses. Traditionally the lotus position is used because it allows the energies within the spine to circulate more freely, which is desirable in puja.

Mudras (gestures) welcome the deity: *svagata* (greeting) and *vandana* (prayerful homage). These can be performed in many different ways, but basically a bow, with the hands brought together, palms and fingers flat against each other, is the mudra of welcome.

The bow is a gesture of recognition and homage. The bow physically focuses us on the pratima.

This mudra connects various *nadis* (nerve pathways) through out our body and brings us to bindu (akasha), a state of balance, by stopping the interplay of tattwas, from which everything is derived in the phenomenal world. It is from the bindu point that everything is created. This mudra helps to align us with the creative matrix of the cosmos and to create a via, or a portal from our physical world into other *lokas* (dimensions of time and space).

Water has four applications: *padya* (water for cleansing the feet), *acamana* (mentioned twice, for sipping and for cleaning the lips), and *snana* (water to bathe the deity). The ritual significance of water to bathe the symbol of the deity and oneself is purification, washing away any intention that is not relevant to the worship. From a magical perspective, water is used to absorb and dissolve irrelevant and inharmonious energy.

Arghya (offerings) usually refers to specific items or money that the sadhaka gives up. The objects should be meaningful to the sadhaka in order for the sacrifice to be effective. Each object sacrificed in this manner results in a closer relationship with the deity.

The concept is the same as the western concept of giving money at Sunday worship. Every worshipper knows that the temple has to be maintained, this is a means to do so. Thus arghya provides the means for the building of structures, and the purchase of items to bring our consciousness closer to our intended purposes. Reproducing the forms of Shiva and Shakti in as many places as possible is a powerful tool, adding meaningful reminders to our lives. A beautiful temple in-forms the mind of the beholder with the inherent vibration of that temple. It is a matter of *vastu*, the large scale use of the magick of form to aid the worshiper.

Food upacharas include *madhuparka* (honey, ghee, milk and curds to feed the deity) and *naivedya* (food for consecration). Tantrics consider food to be full of prana (life energy), so the offerings provide prana or life substance to the deity. Madhuparka helps to create a bridge connecting the inner and outer cosmos so that the deity will manifest for the worshiper in a substantial manner. Naivedya is food put before the deity for consecration. The deity impregnates the food laid at its feet with its essence, then the worshiper eats this food during or after ritual worship to maintain a connection or imbibe certain qualities, characteristics or powers associated with that deity. Naivedya is ritually related to the *apas* tattwa.

Attire upacharas are *vasana* (garment), and *abharana* (ornament) for the deity. Garments are specific colors with symbols signifying the purpose of the deity. Both vasana and abharana symbolize the powers and qualities of the pratima, and communicate these to the sadhaka as the sadhaka interacts with the deity, dressing and adorning them, and gazing on them.

Other ritual elements include *gandha* (sandal paste), *puspa* (flowers), *dipa* (light), and *dhupa* (incense).

Flowers have a dual purpose. They provide prana or energy for the deity and the process of worship, as well as scent and a beauty of form. They are ritually related to the tattwa of *akasha*.

Scents and the nanoparticles formed by burning incense, easily carry information from the physical realm to the quantum realm, and vice versa. This nanotechnology bridges the inner and outer worlds, providing a structure for materialization. Incense, dhupa, is related to the *vayu* tattwa; and sandal paste, gandha, is related to the *prithivi* tattwa.

Light, dipa, is related to the *tejas* tattwa and represents the presence of *vidya* (knowledge) and the wisdom derived from it. Dipa is the symbol of enlightenment and *bhoga* (enjoyment).

Puja to your liking

The upacharas of the classical form of puja need not be followed slavishly. For the most part, intention and focus are what make puja powerful. How this is accomplished can vary according to circumstance. There are many specific practices outlined for puja, but most important is to understand the purpose of the practices, so that rituals can then be tailored that suit ones own desires, needs and circumstances.

The continuing study of Tantric puja can bring you insight into its many facets. If available, a teacher can be a great help; but it is the practice itself which will reveal the most to you by intuition as you connect with the focus of your puja.

Puja need not be an elaborate production. It is more important to do something, however small, with joy, dedication and focus, and make it a regular part of your life. The simple recitation of a mantra on a subway, or the lighting of a candle before dinner, for instance, can be small acts of daily puja.

Part 4
Performing Shiva Shakti meditation

The most powerful and effective Shiva/Shakti meditation is centered on a live and present person to be worshiped (meditated upon) as Shiva/Shakti. For a female sadhaka, the object of meditation would be a nude man, for the male sadhaka, it would be a nude woman.

The two main activities of Shiva/Shakti meditation are classically called *tratak* (steady gazing) and *samadhan* (constant concentration of the mind).

The secret for success in the meditation is to keep bringing your attention back to the landscape of your focus. Stand back mentally and emotionally. Witness the thoughts and emotions that arise, but do not identify with them or give them any more energy; do not start a train of thought or emotion based on what arises. In this way you dissolve your samskaras, so that you can engage in cognition of pure form.

In quantum physics, it is understood that observations are affected by the observer, so the observer must be considered an influence in the analysis of any phenomenon. Your meditations and their results are shaped by your samskaric overlays, which hide the root phenomenon from you in varying degrees. A constant refocusing is necessary to rend the veil of maya, the illusion.

The Taoist concept of *wu wei*, which literally means "do nothing", is helpful in understanding Shiva/Shakti meditation. The Taoist, like the Tantric, contemplates nature, understanding that all form has the Tao as its inner nature. Wu wei means to discern and follow natural form in a completely receptive way.

It is crucial for the sadhaka to like what they are doing and really enjoy ritual puja. The sadhana of Tantra is based on *bhoga*, enjoyment. Each of us has particular keys which open us up to the joy of connecting with Shiva/Shakti. Use those personal elements and integrate them into puja. It is not necessary to have all the components described in the texts about classical puja. One or two will suffice if you understand what you are doing, and they evoke pleasure in you.

Timing

The most auspicious time for the first Shiva/Shakti meditation is new moon, when the sun and moon are conjunct in the sky. This part of the lunar cycle is a maithuna of the sun and moon, represented by a kama-kala triangle consisting of sun, moon and earth.

The sun (*surya/ravi*) is the Shiva principle; and the moon (*chandra/soma*) is the Shakti principle. When they are united in this conjunction/maithuna at new moon, it is easy to absorb the auspicious nature of that maithuna into our consciousness. It is a point of the coming together of the two dynamic principles of the universe, and the coming together creates bindu/akasha, the perfect balance.

Ambience and procedure

Any food or scents used in the ritual should be to your liking. In the temples, all food is eaten by the participants after the ritual, so ritual food offerings should be food that you enjoy eating.

The light should be subdued and the surroundings warm and comfortable. A candle and incense should be lit before the meditation. The person in the role of Shiva/Shakti should be nude and facing the sadhaka, who should also be nude. Usually both take the lotus position. They should be seated a sufficient distance apart so that the whole body of Shiva/Shakti is easily framed in the sadhaka's gaze.

The meditation begins with a mudra. The sadhaka faces Shiva/Shakti and bows with palms together, usually three times for the three lokas. Throughout the meditation this mudra can be used whenever the sadhaka feels the impulse to bow before Shiva/Shakti; and it also brings the sadhaka's mind back to Shiva/Shakti if it should begin to wander.

The meditation should begin with the *japa* (repetitive recitation) of *ha*, the akasha mantra, on the in breath and out breath to balance the polarity within the sadhaka's body, mind, and emotions. This brings together ida (the lunar channel) with the pingala (the solar channel) along the spine, and produces maithuna of Shiva and Shakti within the sadhaka. Thus the microcosmic sun-moon conjunction within the sadhaka, is joined with the macrocosmic sun-moon conjunction.

With Shiva/Shakti seated before them, the sadhaka begins contemplation. Now, what does the sadhaka do during contemplation? Nothing, but look and feel! Simply meditate on the form before you. Do not expect to feel anything, and do not look for anything. Just meditate on the form, nothing else.

During the meditation the sadhaka at intervals can mentally recite the mantra "*Om shakti ah hum*" (Shakti come to me) if male; or, if female "*Om shiva ah hum*" (Shiva come to me).

This contemplation can last for as long as desired. However, one should come to an agreement before puja about how long the puja will be so that all participants will be comfortable and happily engaged for the time period agreed upon. There is no value in lengthening meditations to the point that the participants become physically uncomfortable.

The meditation should close with the sadhaka bowing before the Shiva/Shakti with palms together in mudra.

The sadhaka should not touch Shiva/Shakti during these meditations or have any interaction other than contemplation. If touch or sexual activity occurs, then you will have to regroup at another time and try again.

There are variations in which the participants do touch and feel each other, and circulate their energies together; but that should only occur after several sessions of simple visual contemplation.

Arousal and transmutation

The average person can usually understand sexual arousal, and some can also understand sensual arousal. Sexual arousal is a result of sensual arousal, but in the average person the awareness of the subtleties of sensual arousal is minimized because the experience is immediately felt and responded to in a sexual manner. There is nothing wrong with that per se, but an awful lot is missed in between. For the average person, blood rushes to various organs (as they also do for the sadhaka) and they immediately act upon these sensations according to their samskaras - social norms, customs, personal patterns, etc.

In Shiva/Shakti meditation, the sadhaka responds to the sensual and sexual arousal with no activity but to simply be in the state of arousal and contemplate the form.

It is important in this process that form be transmuted to free energy, and not be brought back into the maze of our preconceived notions and emotions. All the sadhaka's thoughts, emotions, and feelings that arise during the process are put back into the form. Although most of the energies are aroused in the muladhara, svadhisthana and manipura chakras, small residual energies rise up to the complexes we have in the other chakras as well, and we feel, emote, and think about the process and form before us.

The sadhaka does not stop this process and allows the flow of thought, emotion, and feeling. However, as soon as possible, these are rerouted and transformed, as the sadhaka takes these energies and refocuses them back into the landscape of the form. After a while the sadhaka can recycle all the attendant energies back into the form almost immediately. As soon as a thought, feeling or emotion arises, the sadhaka focuses more intently upon the land-scape before them, and thus diminishes the development of further energy created by samskaras. Thought, feeling and emotions are transformed backed into the form, by a constant refocusing. The intent is to feel the form and the energy it evokes without the at-tendant overlay from our samskaras that such a situation normally would give rise to.

Part 5
Kundalini, form and action

Although we all react to form, few of us take time to contem-plate how form brings us to action. To do so allows us to begin to understand our relationship to form and thus to the cosmos.

In the early days of television, it was not unusual for an automo-bile advertisement to contain not only the car but a beautiful wom-an standing next to the car, extolling its fine qualities while rubbing the upholstery in a sensual manner. Madison Avenue advertising executives knew that at that time it was men who bought cars, and that superimposing a sensual form of the opposite polarity on their product would influence men to buy. To the Tantric, the process was quite obvious. The sensual female model raises the kundalini energy of male observers; and as she rubbed the upholstery, the male viewer's sexual energy was transformed into a desire for the car.

It was a powerful and very manipulative way to sell cars. The model not only raised kundalini energy but directed that energy through her gestures into the form the car sellers wanted it to be transformed into.

Since those early days advertisers have become more subtle and sophisticated for the most part, and stimulate sexual feelings in more hidden ways. The advertising industry spends millions of dollars per year, hiring psychologists and teams of workers whose sole job it is to reach the viewer by activating kundalini and mak-ing it take the form they want within you, the perceiver.

In our culture as social creatures, we are surrounded by attempts to stimulate and direct our kundalini energy with layers upon layers of forms that are woven in with more forms. In the constant interplay the real purpose of form becomes so obscured, that most people have no clue that the purpose of form is to enlighten.

Instead of allowing overlays of form to be used to manipulate their energy, the sadhaka contemplates the root form and root forces, and works to break down the associations that our cultural and personal experiences and karma have attached to them. This is achieved by a reduction process that dissolves the forms our perceptual constructs impose on elemental/root forces.

Our emotions and intellect tend to obscure intuition, awareness and true feeling. In the practice of Shiva/Shakti meditation, emotion and intellect are developed, refined and combined to produce spontaneous awareness of the nature of things as they are. To do this, emotions are transmuted into devotion, and intellect transmuted into a yearning for further discovery.

Karma and samskaras

Tantra calls us to step beyond the confines of the karmic mazes that we run daily, and to transform ourselves. Each of us has physical, emotional and mental karma. The Tantric recognizes the limitations created by their own karmic overlays and seeks to develop beyond them.

From birth, each person born has a set pattern through which all energies will circulate. These perceptual constructs, samskaras, unfold as a result of training, experience, and enculturation; they filter kundalini energy and put it into form immediately according to our karma. Most of us are unaware of this process and actually believe that the actions we take, and the feelings we have, are the result of rational thinking based upon experience. In reality, our perceptions are limited according to our karma. The limits to our perceptions can readily be seen in our astrological natal chart.

According to each person's samskaras, a certain portion of the knowledge of form is used to adorn their lives with more form, which is the process of life. But, such actions entrap those involved in an ever recurring round of lila (cosmic play) if they do not really understand what is happening.

We are each endowed by our karma with particular powers and abilities. Such powers as are generally wielded by humans are only the tip of the iceberg and are normally used without understanding the root forces involved. This eventually leads to a crashing transformation which is not understood or controlled by the temporary wielder of that power. Thus, most people become the victims of their own powers. This happens, quite simply because most people only know enough to enhance and develop the capacities that their karma has given them.

In the process of meditation, the sadhaka redirects the energy that would normally be routed through the filters of their samskaras and instead sends it back into the form being perceived. Thus the samskaras are no longer fed or energized in the normal fashion. Instead, the sadhaka realizes a more intimate relationship with the nature of form itself.

To meditate on the landscape of the human body is something very few people do for extended periods of time. Although the practice may sound simple, many difficulties arise. The tendency of the mind is to want to be engaged in performing activities with form, rather than to merely contemplate form.

The sadhaka in practice is ever recycling thoughts and feelings that arise by putting them into the form. This process is sometimes difficult to understand. When a thought, emotion or feeling arises, it is immediately routed to the visual field before the sadhaka; so, all consciousness is transformed back into perceiving the form.

All energy is transmuted back into the form. This requires a sort of cessation of thinking and emoting during the process of contemplation. All becomes form. Usually form evokes a myriad of responses and these responses lead to other responses. Form evokes patterns, trains of thought, and feelings that we follow like Pavlov's dogs. Our samskaras take us further and further away from the initial impetus.

These samskaras, patterns, karma must be dissolved and re-cycled, back into the original elements from which they came; so, again and again we bring ourselves back into the landscape of the form before us. The form reveals our samskaras to us, and as our samskaras are revealed, we let them dissolve back into the form.

As we let go of these karmic patterns we reach stages in which the form reveals its hidden nature to us; aspects that were hidden by the patterns our samskaras have overlaid upon the simplicity before us.

The sadhaka should literally become lost in the landscape of the form. This practice is something a Tantric can do for a whole lifetime and still not realize the full potential of it. It is an art form that leads to enlightenment. Focus and constant refocus is the key to developing this art.

In Shiva/Shakti meditation, the sadhaka lets the human form envelop them with its essence and "in-form" them, gently guiding them into itself and revealing its essence. Great artists understand that form has within it an essence that is beyond words.

One can feel a gentle breeze play upon the body on a hot sunny summer afternoon and relish the delicious sensations of that ex-perience; but it is not easy to express the totality of those feelings with words and intellect. Poets try, but really, the moment is always a private one in its full intensity. That is why Tantrics will exhort you to engage and experience rather than to analyze and describe the union of Shiva/Shakti in meditation. Language can guide, but is it no substitute for the experience itself.

Part 6
Tao, Tea and Art

Shiva/Shakti meditation should be understood as an aesthetic experience.

It is the process of seeing form behind maya, the veil of illusion created by our samskaric energies. This veil obscures the root nature of form. The simplicity and beauty is hidden to us, and thus the meaning and potential of life. We lose our creative root and understanding of first principles. Our samskaras do allow us to analyze and develop theories at the outer margins of superficial phenomenon, but progress toward true enlightenment can only come about with the understanding of first principles, first form.

The *Tao Te Ching* reminds us

"The Tao begot one. One begot two. Two begot three. And three begot the ten thousand things. The ten thousand things carry yin and embrace yang. They achieve harmony by combining these forces."

Within our lives of "ten thousand things" we learn to distill out the essence of form and its dynamics. By combining yin/female and yang/male, enlightenment/harmony occurs. To combine the polarities, the Tantric contemplates and becomes fully receptive to the form of the opposite sex, and becomes in-formed by it.

The tea ceremony is a meditation on the nature of form and its polarity interaction at a deeper social level. The Shiva/Shakti meditation is based on the same principle as the tea ceremony to awaken us to a different level of awareness.

The Urasenke school of Chanoyu (tea) explicitly deals with the coming together and balancing of polar opposites through contemplation of form. The participants, utensils, and the time and space pattern of the ritual all become a form, which is contemplated, experienced and felt. The whole of it is contemplated as one, the Tao. We are led to the one through the subtle process of tea. The different elements of the tea ceremony produce a harmony which is the nature of the Tao, and the result of bringing together the male/sun/yang with the female/yin/moon.

The brazier is yang and the water jar is yin. They must be placed just so, to represent a balance in composition which reflects or harmonizes with the balance of the Tao. The gogyo dana (five element shelf) represents the five tattwas or elements. The guests are considered yin and the host yang.

The tea room itself represents the universe and the interplay of the various combinations of forces and form expressed through the trigrams of the I Ching. The trigrams are all combinations of yin (open) and yang (solid) lines. The tea room is square and has four floor mats divided among the trigrams and a hakke-bon, an eight trigram tray.

It is an art form with a fine aesthetic, and simplicity is the keynote for practice. Rikyu, a 6th century Zen tea master, said, "The way of tea is naught but this: first you boil water, then you make tea and drink it."

If one can understand the concept of the tea ceremony, one can then begin to understand the concept of Shiva/Shakti meditation. In Shiva/Shakti meditation, the participants take off their clothes, sit down and drink in the image.

One does not add to, or subtract from the experience, one just experiences what is. This concept has been well stated in another way by Rikyu, "Though many people drink tea, if you do not know the way of tea, tea will drink you up".

Analogous to the tea ceremony in Shiva/Shakti meditation is the universe represented by the nude human form. The five fingers on each hand and the five toes on each foot represent the five elements in their positive and negative polarities. The two legs and two arms, two eyes, two breasts and two nostrils represent the polarity of sun/moon, Shiva/Shakti, yin/yang. The head and genitals represent the one Tao, the coming together of polarity.

Part 7
Nudity

Though it seems a very simple act, Shiva/Shakti meditation has profound effects and consequences. The removal of clothing is an act fraught with great difficulty for most people. Nudity is generally considered immoral, and/or embarrassing, not something most people would do off-handedly. When a person does remove their clothing in front of others, it is a socially significant act that produces emotion, provokes thought and is likely to result in a wide variety of actions based on those emotions and thoughts. What happens to the average person when confronted with nudity, and why?

Clothing, while appropriate for protection from the elements, or for adornment, also hides or masks our true selves. The fear of nakedness is fear of our own naturalness. Layers of clothing can be seen as layers of samskaras that obscure our nature to ourselves and others.

A person who cannot unclothe themselves in meditation or contemplate the nude body of another person, is not ready for the Tantric experience. It is one of the portals of Tantric initiation.

The puritan and the egomaniac

For instance, a person coming from a strong puritan background where nudity is considered the work of the devil, would be hard pressed to reform their thought and emotional patterns enough to even consider any kind of practice of Tantra. Their karma stops them from proceeding in this direction.

Conventional morality has never been a feature of Tantra. If a person tries, but cannot proceed to this first stage, Shiva/Shakti meditation, they need to consider why they have a strong aversion to such a natural act. Such an aversion is a signpost showing what fears and issues, samskaras, must be worked through before one can proceed on the Tantric path.

There are many reasons people do not feel comfortable around a nude person or being nude themselves. Whatever the reason, it is still a stumbling block to the practice of Tantra. If one cannot perform this simple exercise, one will never be able to practice Tantra at the level of it being a spiritual discipline.

One should not, on the other hand think that just because one can take off one's clothes in front of others, or that one can view a nude without perturbation, that one is a Tantric. This is far from the truth. Nudity is simply one component of Tantra. It is, however, an essential initiation because it symbolizes the sadhaka's willingness to shed the patterns of the past and tread new paths of discovery.

For the average person, participating in social nudity in itself is a powerful act. Much karma is tied up in the shame, sense of power, and egotism centered in our perceptions of the human body and the role the body plays in our lives. Our lives are formatted by these perceptions, layers upon layers of patterns that hide the true beauty of our nature.

Many religious systems promote and rely on feelings of shame, guilt, and fear to perpetuate their cosmological view. These negative feelings are internal mechanisms that regulate people and keep them confined within societal mores. It is indeed, no small thing to step out of line and walk the path of the Tantric sadhaka.

On the other end of the spectrum, there are those who, for ego gratification, wish to take advantage of the Tantric discipline to satisfy themselves and move on, with no intention of entering upon the path. These, like the puritans, do not get very far. They soon find the meditations very boring and they get no ego gratification for their particular pattern of behavior. They are usually puzzled by the behavior of Tantrics and the nature of the practices, and greatly perplexed at how Tantrics control their emotional urges.

In fact, both sides of this moral coin, both the puritan and the egomaniac have much in common. They both feel that they cannot control these energies. One side says, "cover up lest we be led to shameful behavior." The other side says, "I don't care how unaesthetic or gross I am, I'm going to do what I want." Neither will learn much, but they will provide an amusing interplay. Amusing to the Tantric, that is!

They need each other to support their world views. If the gross egomaniac did not have the puritan side to bounce off, what they do would no longer be considered wicked and it would take all the fun out of it. And of course, the puritan needs people who exhibit gross sexual behavior in order to bolster their own belief in the wickedness of it all. They are a dependent polarity pair.

The Tantric, rather than seeing the egomaniacal sensualist as the devil, sees a person out of control who sits down for a drink and can't seem to stop until they are dead drunk, thus much overshooting the mark of a pleasant experience.

The puritan sees the drunk and declares, "See, that substance leads to drunken incoherence and all manner of other ills. Never drink that stuff, it's bad for you as you can plainly see."

Of course both have missed the mark. They both rely on aversion to each other's excessive behavior: not good living, at least from the Tantric point of view.

Neither side likes the way of Tantra, and neither side takes the time to contemplate nudity. One side is too busy avoiding it, and the other side is too busy doing something to it, to ever stop long enough to understand just why they are covering up, or why they are doing it "to it". How strange all this is to the Tantric!

These are two very good ways to destroy nature: deny its existence, or strip mine it into oblivion. Both are acts of denial, immature responses to ourselves and the cosmos. The inhibitions instilled in us by our moral codes create a dance of extremes, a dance that perpetuates dysfunction.

Colonization: hearts and minds

Puritanism has an economic dimension. During periods of colonial expansion, missionaries were sent out alongside the soldiers. After the soldiers conquered the lands of a people, the missionaries proceeded to colonize their minds. They did this by enforcing certain moral codes and behaviors based on European theological concepts, which were inextricably tied into the economic ethos of the conqueror.

In one sense this could be seen as more benign than the alternatives, which were direct enslavement or genocide of the conquered peoples. Colonization, enslavement and genocide did occur in various mixes across the globe as the economic plundering advanced. In any case, the colonizers realized that it was more effective to change the values of conquered populations than to try to otherwise enslave them. In fact, it cost less to do so. Real living armies and police drain the empire's treasury. Instead, colonize the minds of the people with a structure of social concepts (the conqueror's religion). Create silent internal sentinels that cause each conquered person to automatically punish or reward them self according to the new model.

This system would have to be fairly brutally enforced at first, but after time, say a few generations, the conquered culture would be effectively cut off from its own roots and pressed vigorously into the service of the empire's economic demon. The new paradigm, the structure that was imposed on and eventually internalized in the conquered, would allow the wheels of commerce to turn so as to enrich the colonizers. This paradigm or world view, was Christianity.

Religion of exile and the ethic of work

Christianity's creation story is one of exile from paradise, exile from naturalness. Adam and Eve suddenly perceive their own nakedness, feel ashamed and fashion clothes for themselves. The beginnings of the fashion and garment industry you say–yes, but ah, oh so much more. Adam and Eve and all their descendants (from this story) are to forever feel shame at their naturalness and are doomed to work by the sweat of their brow. What a convenient story for the colonizers, as most of the conquered cultures were more naturalistic in their habits and world view and also economically viable, with no need for the angst and turmoil engendered by the story of Adam and Eve, and the imposition of the European work ethic.

The colonizers knew that the peoples they conquered had to be made to feel that the way they lived was wrong, and the way the colonists wanted them to live was right. Most of these conquered societies did not lack commodities to meet the needs of their lifestyles. And, for the most part, work was more nominal and integrated into social life.

The European model was quite different. Discontent needed to be implanted, seeds sown to grow the wheels of commerce. If the people are not discontent with who and what they are, there would be no workers to supply the demands of European ambition.

The seeds of this discontent are feelings of shame about nudity, sexuality and naturalness; and the promotion of the work ethic. When these feelings are evoked, people become distanced from the original form and natural play of kundalini energy. Kundalini, people's life-force, is rerouted into a form that is useful for the empire.

Any inherent human value and validity, a person's intrinsic worth and birthright, if you will, is denied by the colonizers so that they, the colonizers, and their institutions can be the only arbiters of human value and dignity. This makes people a commodity in a market of approval. So, the market of approval becomes defined by those with the resources to inflict harm or induce compliance with other coercive means, subtle and not so subtle.

The redirection of the natural flows and interplay of energy was the job of the missionaries who performed what military people would today call psy-ops (psychological operations). Psy-ops is an arm of the military whose purpose is to create subtle transformations in the psyche of the populace. This is done with a variety of techniques, both interventions and persuasive inducements, to achieve whatever the desired end. If these techniques failed, then good old fashioned force was the norm: if we can't persuade you nicely, we will kill you!

A thousand stories emerge, such as the loss of the language and culture of Hula among the Hawaiian islanders, all sad tragedies that indigenous populations had to suffer at the hands of missionaries and military. James Michener's powerful novel "Hawaii" deals with some of these issues.

The natural interplay of kundalini through form had to be channeled into commodity, supply and demand. The idea of the natural self was supplanted with the idea of the commodity self: your value comes from what you produce, not what you are. For many of the conquered cultures, this paradigm required an in-depth reconstruction of their world view so that an appropriate matrix would be in place to feed the economic greed of European nations.

The missionaries imposed their vision of cosmology and theology and thus changed the daily habits of indigenous people. Concepts of "what is valued" and "what is needed" were changed; and then, the standing army could be replaced by the standing army of silent sentinels called conscience, designed by Europeans to swoop down with condemnation and psychosomatic disorder on any who disobeyed the internal commands.

Paradigm of imposition

To the Tantric, the need to take the resources of others and exploit people in the name of god and Bible is the result of a disordered mind that is not contemplating nature; and lacks inner awareness and the discipline to cultivate inner awareness. It is a childish response to an inner lack of creativity, and is dangerous as it spreads its negative karma to the rest of the world.

Our world views and paradigms create energy flow patterns within our chakras, with set routes and relationships. It is part of our karma to be born into such patterns. But, anyone who seeks enlightenment and freedom from the limitations these paradigms impose must ask "Who has designed this paradigm for me and why?"

It is easy to see the operation of this paradigm of imposition elsewhere, but it is not so easy to see this overlay at work within us. From the moment of birth, an enculturation process shapes our personalities and thought processes. Behaviors that are considered desirable are developed and rewarded; while those that are seen as undesirable are extinguished. The core philosophy or theology of a culture defines what behaviors are desirable or undesirable.

For Westerners that core is the Judeo-Christian tradition, codified in the book called Bible. So, the Adam and Eve story shapes our own lives, and nudity becomes something shameful. In western culture, even people that consider themselves not religious, or consider themselves not affected by the common mores, for the most part, don't "feel right" without their clothes and may be quite alarmed at the idea of social nudity. They may give a variety of excuses like: "I don't feel good about my body image," or "I just don't care to do that," and so on. If that same person grew up in a culture where nudity was not considered a shameful state, they would not be making these excuses. They may consider themselves quite insulated from such programming and believe that they are the generators of their own thoughts, but this is not true. Sadly, they are controlled by a paradigm that is of no particular value to them, but is to the society at large.

The silent sentinels have been installed. If one is honest with themselves they can see through this mechanism and begin the process of recovery to live in a more natural relationship with their surroundings.

The conventional morality of a society is rarely questioned. Few people get to the point of asking "Why? Why is this the way it is?"

Conventional morality is usually accepted as being based on some sort of universal ethic. Each person according to their actions defines their acts as either good or bad according to the paradigm.

If one wishes to explore sensuality or sexuality, for instance, according to the Christian paradigm it is not possible to do this in an open matter-of-fact way. Such exploration without an economic and social commitment - marriage - is taboo. Fornication is a "sin," (in the Christian model a "bad thing"). Thus nudity is also bad as nudity is supposed to lead directly to fornication.

Nudity is a degraded state of being in this context. We come into this world naked, and with the paradigm of "original sin" (traced back to the notorious Adam and Eve story), we are exhorted to cover up and be civilized, to progress to a higher state of being by turning away from our flawed "animal natures".

Both religious institutions and political entities control the process of marriage, through issuing licenses and being authorized to conduct the bonding ceremony itself. Why is this? Why can't two people or more for that matter engage in such activity through their own efforts? Has sex become a controlled substance only available through prescription? Not that sex is the only factor in marriage, but marriage is considered the only officially approved venue for the expression of nudity and sexuality.

If one begins to seriously examine one's own cultural habits and taboos, there is a startling dark figure lurking in the shadows. This dark figure is the maker of maya. One begins to feel uncomfortable with this shadow, which wants to remain dark and unknowable. One begins to see its traces everywhere: a pattern, a gesture, an action, a reaction attempting to overlay the natural patterns before us, and change our perceptions of the real patterns to the patterns of maya.

The enculturation process begins at an early age. The energy flow within our chakras is shaped by this enculturation. The cultural patterns become habits, which make our flow of kundalini energy fit the needs of the institutions of which we are a part due to birth circumstance, our karma.

Each religion has a symbol, each nation has a flag, which is a point of convergence for the energies of its members. A specific pattern is laid, rituals formed, and habitual behavior is cemented into our consciousness and everyday life.

Norms and values are set up with a system of reward and punishment to develop what are considered appropriate behaviors. Appropriate behaviors are those that are seen to further the aims of our cultural institutions. We are taught at an early age that value, dignity and validity can only be bestowed upon us or dispensed to us through the institutions that enculturate us. In order to gain and maintain dignity within a system, the correct axioms must be integrated into our psyche, and we must behave accordingly.

To change our movement within these larger patterns evokes the silent sentinels within us, and draws the attention of others within these institutions. To move beyond these borders, to use kundalini energy for purposes other than to feed these institutions is truly not so easy. A tacit disapproval is usually met with, and coupled with other undesirable phenomenon.

In the western model based on the Bible, any acts that humans perform are only "good" if they further God's plan, according to Christianity. Enjoyment is not part of this plan. The doctrine of original sin, which Augustine based entirely on a highly dubious translation of the apostle Paul's interpretation of the Genesis creation story, made us damaged goods, imperfect; and nudity became the symbol of that imperfection. Adam and Eve had to cover the shame of their bodies.

What is acceptable is to use the body to perform work. Again, this model of work is derived from the creation story which says the descendants of Adam and Eve will eat only by the sweat of their brow. So the template was laid, enjoyment in this life was not a valid human pursuit after "the fall."

The inherent worthlessness of the human body is emphasized in this system, and people are made to feel deeply ashamed about their natural state. Nudity is seen as animal nature, crude, and retro. Thus, to contemplate the naked human body is not acceptable.

With this paradigm we are cut off from the acceptance of ourselves by ourselves, and we are forced to reject our naturalness, our closeness with nature. According to Christianity, all humans have fallen from grace and the only way to regain grace is to avoid our animal nature, cover up and work for the glory of God.

In his inquiry into the effects of religious philosophy on the economic order, social scientist, Max Weber came up with some interesting insights into the interdependence of Puritan Christian faith and market capitalism. Although his analysis was limited to a specific movement and a specific time in history, similar processes have occurred in other circumstances and other times.

Weber's conclusion was that, according to Christianity, it was a Christian's duty to work hard, not for personal gain, but to work hard for God. Work was a divine calling, and financial well being was seen as a sign of salvation, God's favor. Poverty and nakedness were signs of God's condemnation.

The rich in this economic system considered themselves God's chosen people, and thus fit to define what the appropriate work for the glory of God was.

Heathens had to be converted and introduced to the proper economy of things. If they did not convert, they were eradicated so that they would not interfere with the onward march and acquisition of natural resources by God's chosen people.

So, the Christian paradigm is to accumulate form, rather than to commune with form. The relationship between form and perceiver shifts from one of personal relationship to one of accumulator. This paradigm isolates people from the objects they accumulate. Quantity replaces quality. A human's personal worth is equated to the number of objects they have accumulated.

One of the more notorious examples of this twisted philosophy of Manifest Destiny was "Dollar Diplomacy," a term coined for the territorial imperialism of the United States at the end of the 19th century. In explaining why the United States decided to take over the Philippine islands, President McKinley stated, "I am not ashamed to tell you, gentlemen, that I went down on my knees and prayed to Almighty God for light and guidance more than one night. And one night late it came to me this way....There was nothing left for us to do but to take them all and to educate the Filipinos and uplift and civilize and Christianize them, and by God's grace do the very best we could by them as our fellow men for whom Christ also died".

Senator Albert Beveridge responded to McKinley's reasoning for annexation by stating, "We will not renounce our part in the mission of the race, trustee under God of the civilization of the world.... He has marked the American people as his chosen nation to finally lead in the regeneration of the world. This is the divine mission of America... The judgement of the Master is upon us: 'Ye have been faithful over a few things; I will make you ruler over many things.' "

Thus one can see what is termed "civic religion" at work: a curious mix of political endeavor and religion which has been the hallmark of territorial acquisition since the dawn of history. Natural symbols and patterns are replaced and overlaid with other patterns and groups of symbols to use the natives' psychic and physical energy to the benefit of the empire.

Barter and sharing systems, rich in spiritual value and natural connectedness were replaced with a cash economy. The need to commune with nature, and its spiritual significance was replaced by the need for money and commodities, and the need for approval from the Church. Thus, step by step, people are distanced from natural processes and their old symbols.

Cultural transmitters, such as language, rituals, symbols were intentionally destroyed so that native peoples would be isolated from their environment and a new paradigm installed. People no longer owned themselves.

It is no wonder that even today indigenous peoples such as the Hawaiians are very angry about the systematic destruction of the ritual symbolism which was the carrier of their culture. Hawaiians are still trying to recover the hula, after it was nearly annihilated by missionary zeal, in service to the culture of the empire.

This same mechanism can be seen today in the attempted annihilation of Tibetan culture by the Chinese. Although it proceeds from a different paradigm, (the Peoples Cultural Revolution) than the Christian imperialists, the process and results are the same: the total destruction of the spiritual matrix of a culture. The brutal subjugation and marginalization of native Tibetans, the destruction of the monasteries and temples, and the attempt to replace the Dalai Lama's successor with a puppet lama is just another powerful example of the insidious techniques employed to destroy a culture's connection with its soul, its spiritual heritage and close ties with nature.

Every culture has a paradigm, an invisible thought form that must be fed and tended to. It also has boundaries and sentinels. These silent and not so silent mechanisms enforce patterns on individual people's kundalini energy, and also take a portion of peoples' energy to maintain the paradigm.

We are all part of systems that feed upon themselves and have a particular vision of their own future, growth and welfare. Sacrifices are made to these paradigms (god or nation), armies go forth to slaughter and be slaughtered. We are victims of the karma of historic happenstance.

We don't remember where we came from and we do not really know where we are going, because we are not making the choices. Somebody else is.

Tantrics have a historical perspective outlined by a series of *yugas* (ages), and define the age we presently live in as Kali Yuga. The first yuga was Satya Yuga, a golden age of enlightenment.

Arthur Avalon in *Tantra of Great Liberation (Mahanirvana Tantra)* compares the Satya Yuga with the story of Adam and Eve,

"The Garden of Eden is the emblem of the paradisiacal body of man. There man was one with nature. He was himself paradise, a privileged enclosure in a garden of delight".

Then followed the Treta and Dvapara Yugas, characterized by a diminishing understanding of the human relationship to first form, and its role in enlightenment.

The fourth age, Kali Yuga, which is our present age, is considered a dark age dominated by destructive forces. The *Vishnu Purana*, which includes the story of creation, describes Kali Yuga as an age

"...where property confers rank, wealth is a virtue, falsehood is the source of success, and outer trappings are confused with inner religion."

The Tantric perspective that describes the cycle of yugas and the implications of each age, is an indicator of knowledge and understanding of how cultural paradigms reroute and control their member's kundalini energy.

Early Tantrism in India with its natural worship of first form, was suppressed by the brahmins, the ruling caste. The brahmins' Vedic religion was based on priesthood, sacrifice and caste.

Tantrics were opposed to the brahmanic religion and social system, which included sex discrimination and sati. And, Tantrics were vehemently opposed to the caste system. Caste is most readily shown by the clothing a person wears. Nudity is thus a powerful political, social and spiritual statement, and a sign of liberation for all people regardless of caste.

This is why Tantric rituals are performed in the nude.

Pancha Makara

Ritual of the five elements

The ritual of the five elements, also known as the pancha makara or the 5M ritual, consists of sharing food, drink, social and sexual play, and sexual intercourse. This coming together is called a chakra or circle. All activities within the chakra are dedicated to moksha (liberation).

Pancha makara is the Tantric equivalent of a Christian Sunday church service. It can be considered a ritual of worship, but care must be exercised when using the word "worship" in the context of Tantra.

Spiritual adulthood

The opening mantra of this ritual communion is *aum aham brahmasmi*, which means "I am Brahma, the creator." A Tantric, although using external symbols as devices of worship, realizes that ultimately the whole cosmos resides within themselves. So, really, Tantra is not a religion, and Tantric worship is quite different from most religious worship.

"I am Brahma" is a frightening thought for most Westerners. To the Tantric, the average adult is like a new-born child, without much awareness of self or mastery of even the most basic motor skills; but the child will grow to master themselves and the world around them to a much greater degree. Spiritual puberty occurs when an individual gets even the slightest glimmer of the realization "I am Brahma." Spiritual adulthood is a process of maturation into that role. Once an adult has reached spiritual puberty, they are ready to participate in the ritual of the five elements.

Most people need some support to navigate the treacherous waters of maya (illusion). For a child learning to walk, it is helpful to grasp objects in the environment to steady and balance on unsure legs. As a person matures, they outgrow the need for a parent, god or goddess who tells them what to do and how to do it. Religion provides support for the immature. However, as a person matures spiritually, such supports no longer answer a need, and they become impediments to newer and more sophisticated movements in time and space.

The rules laid down by religions are at their best signposts for sane living that help people develop a more open awareness of themselves. At their worst, moral rules are tools of repression that do not allow the free exchange of ideas that result from the natural process of spiritual awakening. Moral dogma has its place for the uncontrolled and the unruly who feel a need to be whacked or sent to hell when they do wrong; or to be rewarded by a heaven when they do what they consider right. To the Tantric this is spiritual immaturity.

At a certain level, moral dogma may serve selfish tribal enterprises well, but it should never be confused with some sort of universal truth. When particular actions become attached to a concept of sin, with attendant reward and punishment, we have begun the journey down the slippery slope, from the Tantric point of view.

Historically, Tantrism is in part a political reaction against the rigid caste system of the brahmins. Buddhism and yoga also have roots in defiance of the tyranny of the rigid moralists of Vedic culture.

Instead of imposed rules and mores, the sadhaka continually develops a more full, visceral awareness of the consequences/karma of any action. Instead of not hitting other people with a stick because of fear of reprisal or punishment, the sadhaka refrains from hitting other people with a stick because the sadhaka can, at a certain level, actually feel the pain of the other person.

The five elements of pancha makara

The pancha makara is the ritual of the five elements: ether (*akasha*), air (*vayu*), fire (*tejas*), water (*apas*), and earth (*prithivi*).

These elements are the building blocks of the universe and have their counterparts in the many *lokas* (spheres) beyond the physical. Each element plays a significant role in our evolutionary pattern and journey of discovery.

The term "five M" refers to the Sanskrit names of the elements - four substances and one ritual act traditionally included in the ritual:

madya	wine	fire
mamsa	meat	air
matsya	fish	water
mudra	parched cereal	earth
maithuna	sexual intercourse	akasha

Pancha makara is based on the role of the five elements in our lives. It channels karmic energies into a positive mode of self expression so that we develop a deeper awareness of the workings of these elements.

Everything tangible in time and space is composed of, and resides within the energy matrix called akasha. From akasha emerges the two polarities fire and water, and their interactions create the elements air and earth. Everything is composed of the five elements; and to direct the flow of these energies leads us to moksha (liberation). Pancha makara is an invitation to awareness and engagement with these energies within our own soul.

To direct the flow of the five primal energies, we need to form a relationship with each of them. To form a relationship there must first be recognition. Recognition begins relationship. Pancha makara is about how the relationships are formed after the first formal recognition. Each element is met within us and outwardly, at both the macrocosmic and microcosmic levels.

The ritual is a physical foundation for expansion of our awareness of our journey through time and space. It leads to a deeper comprehension of the world around us, and gives us the opportunity to design our movement consciously. It is an alchemical ritual that transforms karma with the philosopher's stone of knowledge, wisdom, and experience.

Bhoga, sensuality and moksha

Pancha makara engages the five physical senses, which are related directly to the five elements. Sight, taste, touch, smell, and hearing, are all focused within the chakra (circle) to receive the understanding of that which is.

Before entering the chakra, the participants divest themselves of all former knowledge, opinions, prejudices and worldly trappings to begin anew. As much as possible of the time and space context of our incarnation is left behind. This is represented by the complete nakedness of the participants.

When the ritual is over and the participants step out of the chakra circle, they resume their incarnation with a heightened awareness of purpose.

Pancha makara is a sensual ritual. The sadhaka must accept sensuality as the foundation of our existence; and leave behind denial and guilt about this natural base of being. Recognizing our nature and accepting it allows kundalini energy to flow more freely through our individual chakras. Dedication and intent guide the energies into new forms that will expand our awareness, and lead us in our process of liberation from ignorance.

The decision of an individual to enter the chakra is an initiation, and a spiritual awareness. To consciously dedicate our natural selves to the task of spiritual enlightenment, and to physically act out this dedication in ritual is a powerful tool.

Each initiate enters the circle with a strong sense of, "this is who I am and this is what I do and I dedicate this all to discovery." It is a ritual of sacrifice in that our samskaras are burned up in the flames of desire, so that we are transformed. A phoenix rises out of the ashes.

The transformation does not negate physical sensuality. Instead it leads to a deeper understanding and appreciation of it and its connection to the ultimate source of being. Sensuality for the sadhaka is both a stepping stone to enlightenment and enlightenment itself, once the veil of ignorance is removed.

Enlightenment is a matter of perspective. Attitude/perspective cannot be emphasized enough in Tantric sadhana, and, of course, in pancha makara. The participants' attitude should be joyful, free and peaceful - *bhoga* (enjoyment). The ritual should be approached with sensuality and delight, and a full awareness of what makes us feel good: pleasant sights, pleasant sounds, pleasant touch and feeling, pleasant tastes and pleasant sexual intercourse.

In Tantra the enjoyment of the senses is a spiritual act in and of itself, so there is no need to justify sensuality. It is the natural flow of the interplay of the elements; and it is what brings us to an expanded awareness of the universe, and thus liberation from *avidya* (ignorance). *Vidya* (knowledge) is gained by acceptance of our sensual nature and dedication (intention).

Bhoga is the needle on the compass that guides the sadhaka. The intent of Tantric ritual such as pancha makara is for the sadhaka to tune in to joy and wonder that is so fully engaging that the sadhaka's ego-self recedes in the sadhaka's consciousness.

Participation in a chakra circle clears the chakras of each participant. Repressed subconscious energy is freed from the various complexes, samskaras, tied up in the chakras. Kundalini can then freely flow up the chakras and back down again in a grand circulation, unimpeded by energy-sucking complexes and obsessions.

Each participant must realize the importance of divesting themselves of their impregnation by the culture they grew up in. Each culture or subculture has laws, rules, regulation or morals which include various sanctions and taboos. Some of these may be rational and relevant while others may not.

For instance, it is generally considered immoral for married people to have sex outside of their marriage. In our society, this is usually grounds for divorce. To a Tantric this is not a moral problem. The Tantric sadhaka can choose to walk outside the moral bounds society has created.

To step into the chakra circle is to turn one's back on convention and commune with the creative matrix of all being. This requires courage and is why in classical literature the Tantric is called the *vira* (hero), a very important Tantric concept. The vira is one who can step out above and beyond the crowd, lead, take chances and discover new things. Tantric sadhana is not for the faint of heart.

अ

Stepping out of psychological and other confines is not easy for most people. Humans like to follow their set patterns. They will generally run their accustomed mazes, never thinking to try a different approach, or consider climbing out of the maze entirely. And so it goes.

The Tantric steps out of the maze. To step into the chakra circle is a powerful statement. It is a statement that says, "I want to see beyond the walls! I want to see why those walls were there in the first place, what was their meaning and purpose."

Performing the ritual

A pancha makara is the social center piece for Tantra yoga. The ritual can be performed at any time, but most formally it is performed on the day of the new moon, or about seventy two hours after the new moon.

The ritual is simple. To open the ceremony, a circle, real or imaginary, is drawn with a wand, a hand or other object. The circle can also be drawn by sprinkling salt in a circle. All ritual activity will take place within this circle, so it should be drawn large enough to contain all the participants and their activities within its periphery. The number of people in attendance can be from one to as many as you like.

As mentioned before, the four substances and one ritual act traditionally included in the ritual are:

madya	wine
mamsa	meat
matsya	fish
mudra	parched cereal
maithuna	sexual intercourse.

Each of the food substances represents one of the elements: fire, air, earth, water; and the act of sexual intercourse represents akasha.

Each sadhaka partakes of each of the food elements, and engages in maithuna within the circle. The four substances and the sexual act can all have substitutes. Any food or drink can be substituted for the food materials and an offering of flowers or any gesture of union of Shiva and Shakti can be substituted for the ritual sexual intercourse.

Each participant ritually bathes before attending the circle, and all participants enter the circle naked. Within the circle, the participants share and enjoy the first four Ms. After the four Ms have been consumed, each couple within the circle engages in foreplay and concludes with maithuna. At all times within the circle and engaging in any activity, the sadhaka dedicates each and every action to moksha.

Pancha makara can be as sophisticated or as simple as you like. If you are one person, you simply enter the circle, sit comfortably, partake of the four Ms and then meditate on union with the cosmos.

Raising the Kundalini: Bhuta Shuddhi

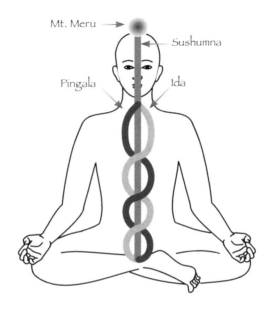

The royal road, or pathway to liberation, is situated along the spine. Tantric sadhana is to follow this pathway to the top of Mt. Meru. The tip of Mt. Meru is the sahasrara chakra, located above our heads. Mt. Meru is *merudanda*, center of the universe. This merudanda is the bindu point of every mandala and yantra. The road itself is called *sushumna*. Running along sushumna on the spine are the *pingala* and *ida* channels for the solar and lunar currents, respectively. The solar is the yang or electric male energy, and the lunar is the yin or magnetic female energy. These pathways intersect and form chakras along the spine.

In Tantric lore there is a Shiva form (yang) and Shakti form (yin) assigned to each chakra. It is the lila (interplay), of these two, the electric and magnetic forces, that manifest the universe or what is referred to as maya (illusion).

Within sushumna is a finer passageway called *vajrini*, and within vajrini is an even finer passageway called *chitrini*. These three pathways are referred to as *tribindu* or three footed god.

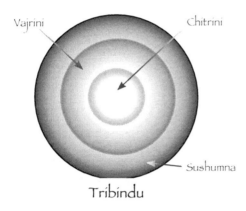

Tribindu

The sushumna, vajrini, and chitrini represent different gradations of the akasha principle within the causal sphere. This tribindu is represented by the mantra aum. A represents the physical plane, U represents the astral plane, and M represents the spiritual/mental plane.

Shakti as kundalini resides in the *muladhara* chakra at the base of the spine. The main practice of Tantric sadhana is to raise the kundalini through the chitrini to the *sahasrara* chakra, in other words, up the length of the spine to above the crown of the head.

The technique for accomplishing this is to sound specific *bija* (seed syllable) mantras either silently or aloud in each chakra, beginning at the muladhara and ending with the sahasrara.

In traditional practice, the sadhaka sits in the lotus position and faces either east or north: east during the day and north at night. A cross-legged position has advantages in that it encourages a straight spine and deep breathing, and spreading the thighs helps open the muladhara chakra. However, kundalini can be raised facing any direction and in any comfortable position: lying down, sitting in a chair, or even walking. You can also practice in bed as you go to sleep or just before getting up in the morning.

Although there are eight major chakras, only six are used for raising the kundalini. The two not included are *ajna*, the sun chakra between the eyebrows; and *chandra*, the moon chakra at the back of the head in the soft part of the skull. Ajna and chandra come together of their own accord when the akasha bija is intoned in the *vishuddha* chakra, at the throat. A bridge is formed between ajna and chandra, and they become one with akasha.

Forming a template

Before you work with the techniques given below, you need to form a template for the kundalini by learning each bija mantra within its chakra, so that the bija, the location of the chakra, and the feel of the chakra are all one memorized unit for you.

To begin, physically chant a seed syllable, feeling that it is located in its chakra. Then, whisper the seed syllable in the chakra, and finally, silently/mentally intone the seed syllable within the chakra. Intoning the seed syllables in this fashion in each chakra will help to awaken kundalini and help to prepare the path of its ascent.

When actually working with raising the kundalini you will intone each mantra (seed syllable) silently in the mind.

Each element has particular qualities.

The **earth element** has a cohesiveness, and weight and density. It feels heavy. The color of this element is usually visualized as anywhere from yellow to brown or black. Soil varies in its color from area to area, and you can choose the color of the soil you are used to.

The **fire element** is active and expansive and is felt as heat. It is seen as light and is usually visualized as red.

The **water element** is contractive and feels cool. It is usually visualized as green.

The **air element** is very light, and uplifting. It negates the heaviness of gravity. The element of air is usually visualized as sky blue.

The **akasha element** feels all pervasive, you are able to be everywhere at the same time. It is usually visualized as a ultraviolet, violet, or purple color.

In practice, for example, the sadhaka intones the mantra *ra* for the element of fire, while visualizing the color red and feeling the heat from the fire element.

Although not necessary, adding color and feeling has advantages in sadhana. The sadhaka literally becomes one with each element, and so has a more wholistic feeling and understanding; and, hence, control of the element.

Chakra yantras

A good way to get acquainted with the elements and energy in a chakra is to meditate on each chakra yantra. Yantras are diagrams of particular energy patterns, and can be used in may different ways.

The simplest way to use the yantras is to sit with the yantra in front of you, and while concentrating your vision on it, audibly or silently intone the mantra over and over. Use the illustration on page 108 for the location of each chakra on the spine, and feel each chakra in your body as you meditate on the yantra.

Following are line drawings of the yantras for each chakra, in order, starting at the base of the spine and ascending to above the crown of the head. You can also view color versions of the yantras at www.tantrayoga.us/yantras.html as well as other sources online.

The seed syllables are pronounced with a short a as in "another."

Muladhara

Element ~ Earth

Bija tattwa mantra ~ La *"luh"*

Colors ~ Browns

Planet ~ Saturn

Svadhisthana

Element - Water

Bija tattwa mantra - Va *"vuh"*

Colors - Green

Planet - Jupiter

Manipura

Element - Fire

Bija tattwa mantra - Ra *"ruh"*

Colors - Red

Planet - Mars

Anahata

Element - Air

Bija tattwa mantra - Ya *"yuh"*

Colors - Sky Blue

Planet - Venus

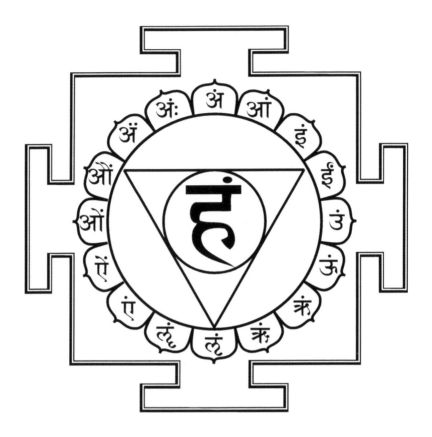

Vishuddha

Element ~ Akasha

Bija tattwa mantra ~ Ha *"huh"*

Colors ~ Violet

Planet ~ Mercury

Sahasrara

Bija mantra - Aum

For a more full engagement, sit comfortably, set the chakra yantra of choice before you and stare at it, visually concentrating for three to five minutes.

Close your eyes and transfer your consciousness to its chakra along your spine.

Transfer your consciousness with the chakra into the yantra.

When your consciousness is comfortably seated within the yantra, repeat the seed syllable for that chakra silently in the mind. You can also visualize the color and feeling of the element while intoning the mantra. Realize at all times that you and the yantra are one. You can remain in the yantra as long as you wish.

When finished, move your chakra and consciousness from the yantra back into your body and open your eyes.

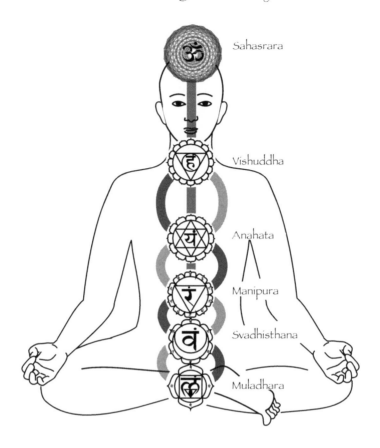

Raising kundalini

To awaken kundalini, first, inhale and draw the energy from all your extremities into a ball of light into the muladhara.

Then, transfer your consciousness to each of the chakras in sequence, beginning with the muladhara (la) at the base of the spine. In each chakra, intone the bija seed syllable (tattwa mantra) once for the chakra, then rise up to the next. After you complete the cycle with aum in the sahasrara, return to the muladhara chakra (la) and begin another cycle. Repeat as many times as you can, and practice this routine on a daily basis.

This is the only ritual you need to perform as a Tantric to ensure your liberation.

Variations on the fundamental technique

You can integrate the cycle of bija mantras into your normal breathing cycle. For instance, move upward through all the chakras from muladhara (la) to sahasrara (aum) on the in-breath, and feel the in-breath raising your consciousness upward through each chakra. As you pass through each chakra, intone its mantra. When you reach the sahasrara, let your breath out while retaining your consciousness in that chakra. When you are ready to take another breath, drop your consciousness to the muladhara and repeat the cycle for as many times as you can.

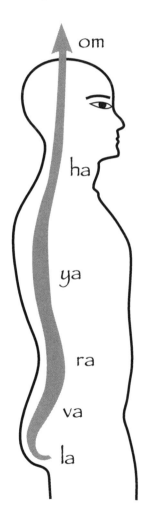

Another variant is to rise to the vishuddha (ha) on the in-breath intoning the bija in each chakra, and then breath out and move upward into the sahasrara as you exhale and pronounce "aum." Then, return to the muladhara and repeat the cycle.

The Shiva Shakti meditation can be combined with raising the kundalini through the chakras with these seed syllables. When you are sitting before Shiva/Shakti, kundalini is easily raised beyond the svadhisthana chakra because of the extra impetus derived from the form before you. As you are stimulated by the form, the energy can be moved up the spine with the seed syllables to the sahasrara.

The akasha sushumna bija mantra can be attached as a prefix to each tattwa mantra when raising the kundalini. In other words, intone *hala* in the muladhara, *hava* in the svadhisthana and so on, placing the akasha bija *ha* before each tattwa mantra as you go up the spine. This brings the consciousness to sushumna and balances the chakras. As each chakra is balanced, a gate is opened in the sushumna so that the energy can easily rise up to and through the next chakra. All of the complexes and actions that derive energy from a particular chakra are transmuted back into akasha so that they are no longer obstacles for the ascent of kundalini through the chitrini to the sahasrara.

Refining karma

All of the techniques discussed in this chapter are called bhuta shuddhi or tattwa shuddhi, which means refinement of the five elements. What happens is that the sadhaka raises their consciousness by reversing the downward manifestation of the five elements within their sphere of sensation.

Each of our chakras has an elemental impulse and connection with one of the five senses, and there are particular karmas associated with it. We can either go through the karma, or we can refine the experience through mantra *siddhi*, or other magical practices. Manifestation, coagula, occurs in a downward direction, from sahasrara to muladhara. By reversing the process of manifestation, solve, we discover the nature of each element and its role in producing the karma in our lives.

It is this untangling of karmic energies that creates auspicious circumstances and better fortune in our lives.

This should not be confused with running away from life. The karmic energy is not suppressed or blocked. It is instead redirected into a new form.

Each time kundalini rises to the sahasrara, it brings a small portion of your consciousness with it to the sahasrara, and in the sahasrara that bit of consciousness becomes enlightened. Like a refreshing rainfall, enlightened bits of consciousness filter down through the chakras to the muladhara and begin to transform your world. It is a gradual process, but there are subtle effects that are immediately noticeable.

Once kundalini is taken up to the sahasrara, the energy can be directed to coalesce as the sadhaka wishes. In other words, the descending elements in the kundalini can be designed and impregnated with new ideas and movements.

A new template for the flow of these energies is constructed with the five elements, as in all other Tantra ritual. This reconstruction is aided by the exalted vibrations of the sahasrara. In this way the template for the sadhaka's life becomes harmonized with the cosmos.

These are the best techniques to raise the kundalini. Since they are gradual, they do no harm to the system. They integrate consciousness on all planes of existence, and give you the increasing capability to refine and transmute your karma. This should be practiced daily and for as long as you can do it without discomfort or time constraints. It is not possible to do this exercise too much: the more, the better.

There are books and teachers that state that raising kundalini is dangerous. This is true if the methods used are not very good. If you use the techniques given here you will find that raising the kundalini is a very smooth and positive experience. It is subtle and occurs over time, This is as it should be, as the body and mind need some time to adjust to the transmutation of consciousness. Raising the kundalini should feel good.

As you work with these practices to raise the kundalini you will notice that you develop what are called siddhis (magickal powers). It is important to stay within certain bounds when working with these capabilities. There is nothing wrong with having or developing these capabilities. Just remember that they can be powerful distractions, and can become hindrances to your well-being if you are not also working to balance out your personality to some degree.

If you follow this practice on a daily basis, you will become more aware of your own personality traits and motivations, and thus more inclined to weed out what you don't like about yourself. Your personality will become more refined and balanced.

You will also grow in knowledge and power, which will help you help yourself as well as others in their journeys. All knowledge and wisdom is contained within your higher self. Raising the kundalini will allow you to better access this.

Tantra does not define a goal. Where you want to go is revealed to you through your practice. As a Tantric sadhaka, the best qualities of all spiritual practices will become available to and through you.

अ

I sent my Soul through the Invisible,
Some letter of that After-life to spell:
And by and by my Soul return'd to me,
And answer'd "I Myself am Heav'n and Hell."

Rubaiyat Of Omar Khayyam

Astrology & Tantra

The study and understanding of auspicious timing of activity is the province of *jyotish*, astrology. Although astrological understanding is not necessary for progress on the Tantric path, it is taken for granted that the sadhaka will avail themselves of knowledge available in this discipline to some degree.

In India it is common to employ astrology for timing even every-day duties. Contemporary mantra manuals delineate lunar and planetary positions, days of the week, and hours, for the practice of mantra.

Any new venture by a Tantric is generally guided by astrological indicators and/or the advice of a guru.

For the Tantric, astrology is considered a tool and guide. The possibilities and tendencies brought to light by astrological study are never regarded as inescapable fate. Noting the energy flows indicated by various planetary positions is very much like getting a weather report. You take the probable weather conditions into consideration as you plan your activities. If you know it is very likely to rain, you can put out a rain barrel, instead of hanging out your laundry to dry, and you will get more benefit more easily from the energy you expend. Working against the cosmic tide can be stressful, just as driving on icy roads is a more difficult experience than driving on clear roads, and more likely to have outcomes (sliding off the road) that are not intended or desired.

Solar, lunar and other planetary positions are indicators of energy flows that have a profound effect on the breath, mind, body, and emotions. These effects mostly go unnoticed by the average individual, but the sadhaka cultivates increasing sensitivity to the characteristic feel of these astrological aspects, to the nature of the energy patterns associated with them, and to their effects in the physical world. From this, the sadhaka understands to use particular moments in time and movements in space to enhance their efforts.

For a beginner, it can save a lot of time and energy to use astrology to choose auspicious moments that will lead to success sooner and bypass a slower trial and error process.

The application of astrological knowledge to Tantric practice can be quite complex and detailed, or be minimal, depending on the abilities and personality of the sadhaka or their guru.

The most significant astrological factors for the practice of Tantra are the positions of the sun and moon. Of all these, the conjunction of the sun and moon, the new moon, is the most important astrological consideration for the sadhaka.

Other important points are the vernal equinox when the sun presides at 0° Aries; and sunrise and sunset, with the various tattwas that occur during the day based upon the times of sunrise-sunset.

The sun, *ravi*, represents Shiva and the pingala channel on the right side of the spine; and the moon, *chandra*, represents Shakti and the ida channel on the left side of the spine. So, the sun and the moon represent the two great polarities that are to be combined in the practice of maithuna.

During the course of the lunar month the relationship of the sun and moon and the earth produces a flow of nerve currents within the human body along the ida and pingala channels to produce different physical, psychological, and esoteric effects that can enhance or diminish the success of various activities. These nerve currents at different times of the solar and lunar cycles also affect different portions of the body through the *nadis* (esoteric prana channels in the body).

Such texts as *The Ananga Ranga* go into great detail about the effects of these subtle currents related to the art of making love and the various parts of the body that should be stimulated at a given time.

Complex astrological divisions of the times of day that possess the qualities of the various tattwas can be found in such works as Rama Prasad's *Nature's Finer Forces*.

There is a wealth of very detailed literature that provides minute analysis of astrological positions and the performance of various ritual meditations. It should, however, be understood that the performance of any act of Tantra is auspicious at any time it is performed. The quality of the ambient space-time matrix may not be as favorable at one time as at other times, or as conducive to immediate success, but the performance of any Tantric ritual will, by the mechanism of cause and effect, lead to success sooner or later.

Lunar cycle

Each segment of time and space has its karma, and affects the flow of energy and the forms the energy will take. New moon, called maithuna, is auspicious for any Tantra sadhana. At new moon, the forces flowing in the ida and pingala channel readily unite in the center of the spine, the chitrini channel, and create bindu (balance). Under these conditions kundalini can rise with great ease.

Bindu has the nature of akasha tattwa, devoid of time and space restrictions as we experience them, so energy can flow freely from one point to another without restriction. The akasha principle is the interconnectedness of all things, so any act performed during an akasha tattwa will bear the fruits of the knowledge of the interconnectedness of all things. During akasha tattwas the ajna chakra can combine most readily with the chandra chakra in maithuna. Bindu is the moment of coming together - a point of balance wherein the two halves of our selves are in communion without one dominating the other. Right brain and left brain form a whole, so our creativity is at a maximum.

At new moon a pathway, free of karmic obstacles, opens to cosmic consciousness from the root muladhara chakra all the way up to the sahasrara. Thus, at this time it is easy for the sadhaka to ascend to the top of Mt. Meru via the chitrini, the very center of the spine, wherein akasha resides.

As the moon progresses from new to full, the benefits of the sadhana at new moon become more apparent. *Amrita* (nectar of the gods) is released and bathes the nadis with its essence. Knowledge and inspiration come into full form by the full of the moon.

The fruits of the sadhana performed at new moon are then offered at full moon to further realization. Each form that comes into being for the sadhaka - mental, emotional, physical - is then sacrificed from full to new. The forms are not discarded or destroyed. They are offered as the base for realization in the coming cycle

From the full moon to new moon the sadhaka prepares by ritual and meditation for the coming new moon.

This constant cycle of renewal and regeneration occurs on a monthly basis, each cycle building upon the previous, and in increments the sadhaka moves closer and closer to their goal.

The term sacrifice here does not mean giving up anything. It is recognition of the ever flowing, ever changing Tao. It is taking the old and creating something new with it. It is transformation and transmutation, a constant dissolving and reforming, the alchemists' solve et coagula formula. It is recycling of cosmic energies.

Annual and daily cycles

The daily and yearly cycles have similar patterns of energy flow. On a daily basis, at both sunrise and sunset, the akasha tattwa dominates, so these are both auspicious times of the day to meditate and perform rituals.

In the yearly cycle the quarter points - vernal equinox (sun entering Aries), autumnal equinox (sun entering Libra), winter solstice (sun entering Capricorn) and summer solstice (sun entering Cancer) are auspicious times for ritual.

These basic cycles are the most important ones for Tantric practice. The three types of lunar and solar cycles - year, month and day - include plenty of opportunities for the sadhaka to get acquainted with and use various astrological tides to provide an ease of working.

Planetary cycles

Traditionally, astrological timing and symbolism is used throughout Tantric practice. There are yantras (mandalas) drawn at specific times relating to particular planets and the energies and forms they represent to aid the sadhaka in their quest. Various mantras are used to ameliorate or accentuate planetary forces that reside in the chakras.

For the western student of Tantra, it is advisable to study some current astrological texts to get at least a general idea of the effects and meaning of planetary movements. This, although not necessary, will give the student an understanding of themselves and their personal karma, and how to work with their natal talents and liabilities in the process of Tantric sadhana.

The Tantric does not view the movement of planetary bodies as the cause of this karma or that. The movements are signposts of energies present within each person. They are indicators of how energy is flowing, not the source of the energy. They are already present within us. Because everything is connected in time and space, it is possible to understand the flow of vital forces through the art and science of astrology. The macrocosm reflects the microcosm.

PLANET	CHAKRA		PLANET	CHAKRA
Saturn	muladhara		Mercury	vishuddha
Jupiter	svadhisthana		Moon	chandra
Mars	manipura		Sun	ajna
Venus	anahata			

With an understanding of astrology you can observe inharmonious aspects between planets, and alleviate the stress from the aspects directly.

This is achieved by meditating with specific mantras in the appropriate chakras. The text *Ancient Hindu Astrology For The Modern Western Astrologer* by James T. Braha includes the planetary mantras. There are also astrological programs such as Day Watch by Matrix software that contain East Indian *tithis*. Tithis are based on the relationship of the sun and moon, and are used to select auspicious times to perform pujas. Day Watch includes planetary hour functions which can also be used to select auspicious times for puja and other activities. To use the planetary hours, you need a basic understanding of each planet from an occult point of view.

There are also other jyotish (East Indian astrology) programs available on the net. Some are free and some can be obtained for a moderate fee. Do an internet search on the term jyotish to find resources for East Indian astrology.

It is not necessary to work with the East Indian astrological format even though Tantra is of East Indian origin. Both Western and Eastern systems of astrology work equally well; it is a matter of personal preference.

For the basics of western astrology *Llewellyn's New A To Z Horoscope Maker And Interpreter* and *The Modern Text-Book Of Astrology* by Margaret Hone are good broad references. There are also many other fine books about astrology available.

Tattwas and planetary hours

The cycles of the tattwas (five elements) are another consideration for timing in Tantric practice. The day is divided into 30 *gharis* from sunrise to sunset and 30 gharis from sunset to sunrise. Each ghari is ruled by one of the five elements - akasha, air, fire, water, earth; in that sequence - from sunrise to sunset. The cycle begins again at sunset with the same sequence. Each ghari lasts for roughly 24 minutes, but of course, the length varies according to the exact time of sunrise and sunset.

To calculate which tattwa (element) is in force at any given time, look up the times of sunset and sunrise for the day in question. This exact times of sunrise and sunset for your location for a particular day, or for an entire year can be found at the U.S. Naval Observatory web site.

To use the data to calculate tattwas (elements) simply figure out how many minutes it is between sunrise and sunset for that particular day. Divide this into 30 sections and you will have the length of each ghari. The first ghari (at sunrise or sunset) will be akasha. This is followed in order by air, fire, water, and earth. This sequence repeats itself until sunset. At sunset, you begin again with akasha followed by air, fire, water, and earth as during the day. For the whole day you would have twelve sets of Tattwas.

The tables mentioned above can also be used to calculate planetary hours if you do not have an astrological program that has this feature.

Planetary hours are calculated from sunrise and sunset, but the sequence of the planets depends on the day of the week. For instance, the Sun rules Sunday and so the first planetary hour would be ruled by the Sun. On Monday the first planetary hour would be the Moon, because Monday is ruled by the Moon. Similarly Saturn rules Saturday, Venus rules Friday, Jupiter rules Thursday, Mercury rules Wednesday, and Mars rules Tuesday.

The sequence of the planetary hours always runs like this: Sun ☉, Venus ♀, Mercury ☿, Moon ☽, Saturn ♄, Jupiter ♃, Mars ♂. Each day starts at sunrise with the planet of the day and moves through the sequence. Unlike the gharis, the sequence continues through sunset and does not begin anew. To calculate the length of each planetary hour, calculate how many minutes there are from sunrise to sunset and divide this number by twelve. The night hours are calculated the same way, except using the minutes from sunset to sunrise to create twelve divisions. Thus, there are 24 planetary hours in a day.

There are many other astrological calculations that can be helpful to the sadhaka, if they are so inclined.

It is not necessary to apply astrological timing to Tantric practice but it can be very helpful much as swimming with the tide makes progress easier.

Glossary

Aham	That which is within.
Akasha	The fifth element, ether, which is the source of the other four elements air, fire, water and earth.
Apas	Water element.
Apsara	Female spirits of the clouds and waters. A personification of a natural force.
Asana	A pose, a position in hatha yoga.
Avidya	Ignorance.
Bhupura	The base upon which the yantra is drawn, a frame.
Bindu	Point or dot. That in which everything resides. A point of balance, center point.
Brahma	The creator.
Brahman	The essence of all things, the ultimate substrate.
Brahmin	Usually refers to one born into the highest cast, however the title should be reserved for those who realize that they are spirit. The roots of the word have nothing to do with social status.
Budha	The planet Mercury ☿ .
Caste system	Most simple version: priests are brahmins, warriors are kshatriya, merchants are vaishya, and artisans are shudras. Very rigid East Indian social system.
Chakra	Literally, wheel. A step-up and step-down transformer of energy. Subtle energy center. The major chakras are located along the spine, and are muladhara, svadhisthana, manipura, anahata, vishuddha, ajna, chandra, and sahasrara.
Chandra	The Moon ☽ .
Circle	Representation of all manifestation.

Deva	A celestial being. A personification of a natural force .
Elements	Akasha (ether), tejas (fire), vayu (air), prithivi (earth), and apas (water) comprise the five elements which are the building blocks for everything in the universe.
Ghari	A specific tattwa time period that is calculated from sunrise and sunset times.
Guru	The planet Jupiter ♃ .
Ida	Spinal current of subtle energy that starts on the left side, and is magnetic, receptive, yin, related to the Moon and water.
Idam	The manifest universe: that which is without
Initiate	One who has a path open to them.
Kama Kala Triangle	A triangle representing space and time.
Kuja	The planet Mars ♂ .
Kundalini	Spinal energy current. Represented as a serpent, which normally lies dormant, coiled around a lingam within the triangle of manifestation.
Lila	The play of the universe, or universal play.
Lingam	Penis, dick.
Madya	Wine.
Maha Mudra	See Maithuna.
Maithuna	Intercourse. A coming together of polarities.
Mamsa	Meat.
Mantra	Magick words.
Matsya	Fish.
Maya	Time and space and what transpires in time and space on all planes and dimensions.
Merudanda, Mt. Meru	The axis of the universe, the spine. The summit of Mt. Meru is the sahasrara chakra.
Moksha	Liberation.

Mudra	Gesture. Also, parched cereal used in pancha makara ritual.
Pingala	Spinal current of subtle energy that starts on the right side of spine, and is electric, active, yang, and related to the Sun and fire.
Prithivi	Earth element.
Puja	Worship, but not to be confused with the Western concept of worship.
Ravi	The Sun ☉.
Sadhaka	One who practices, magician.
Sadhana	The practice, the path.
Samskaras	Habits from the past, prior lifetimes and this lifetime, that can interfere with moksha in your present life.
Sani	The planet Saturn ♄.
Shakti	Female principle.
Shastra	Spiritual text.
Shiva	Male principle.
Siddhi	Magickal powers derived from Tantra sadhana.
Sukra	The planet Venus ♀.
Sushumna	The balance of ida and pingala, Sun and Moon, fire and water. Sushumna has the nature of akasha and bindu.
Tantra	To weave.
Tattwas	see Elements.
Tejas	Fire element.
Temple	A template of the cosmos for performing ritual.
Trataka	Gazing at an object to promote concentration.
Vama Marga	The left-hand path.
Vamacharins	Followers and teachers of the left-hand path, magicians.
Vastu	The magick of form, especially buildings and their surrounds, very much like the Chinese practice of Feng-Shui.

Vayu   Air element.

Veda   Four Vedas - Rigveda, Samaveda, Yajurveda,
                  Artharvaveda - ancient texts that are the
                  primary scriptures of Hinduism.

Vidya   Knowledge.

Vira   Hero. One who overcomes limitations and fears by sacrificing
                  conventional comfort and approval for freedom of the soul.

Vishnu   The preserver.

Vishvasara Tantra
                  Tantric text that includes, "What is here is elsewhere;
                  what is not here is nowhere," or paraphrased "What is
                  here is there, what is not here is not there." (*Om yadihasti
                  tadanyatra yannehasti natatkvachit*)

Yantra   Diagram representing a cosmic force or principle to be
                  meditated upon. Literally means instrument or machine
                  that holds a concept (force/form) within it.

Yoga   To unite, the process of becoming one with.

Yoni   Vagina, pussy.

Bibliography

The Serpent Power: The Secrets of Tantric
      and Shaktic Yoga
      by Arthur Avalon; Dover Publications, Inc. 1974.

Tantra of the Great Liberation: Mahanirvana Tantra
      by Arthur Avalon; Dover Publications, Inc. 1972.

The Tantric Tradition
      by Agehananda Bharati; Rider & Company 1965.

Tools for Tantra
      by Harish Johari; Destiny Books 1988.

Tantra: The Way of Action: A Practical Guide
      to Its Teachings and Techniques
      by Francis King; Destiny Books 1990.

Tantra Yoga: Hindu And Tibetan
      by J. Marques-Riviere; Rider & Company 1970.

Lights on the Tantra
      by M.P. Pandit; Ganesh & Co. 1963.

Tantra: The Indian Cult of Ectasy
      by Philip Rawson; Thames And Hudson 1984.

Tattwa Shuddhi
      by Swami Satyasangananda; Yogi Pulications Trust 1984.

Serpent in the Sky
      by John Anthony West, Quest 1993.

A History of Yoga
      by Vivian Worthington; Arkana 1989.

Namarupa: the Magic of Tantra Mantra

by Phillip Hurley & Leigh Hurley

Namarupa is an initiation into mantra yoga, complete with detailed Sanskrit pronunciation, alphabet and calligraphy guides. All mantras are presented in Devanagari script with English transliteration for easy reference. Written from the perspective of the tantric sadhaka (practitioner), Namarupa presents the esoteric meanings and uses of the mantras and alphabet; and discusses mantra sadhana both as classically practiced and updated for modern life. Of special interest are detailed Tantric mantra techniques for raising kundalini, previously available only to initiates.

Namarupa: the Magic of Tantra Mantra includes:

ॐ Sanskrit letter portraits

ॐ Sanskrit quick reference tables & pronunciation guide

ॐ How to initiate a mantra

ॐ Japa, pranayama, and modes of chanting

ॐ Detailed discussion of bija mantras

ॐ Timing & rectification of mantras

ॐ Deity, planetary, directional & general mantras

ॐ Mantra cycles for working with the five elements and raising kundalini

ॐ Likhita japa and calligraphy guides

www.tantrayoga.us

Herbal Alchemy
by Phillip Hurley

When originally published in 1977, Herbal Alchemy broke new ground as the first straight-forward written presentation of Alchemy in a complete, practical form - as science, art, technique, philosophy, magic and spiritual practice. In this revised and updated edition, Phillip Hurley provides detailed information about the preparation of alchemical elixirs from plants, the application of astrology to herbalism, and reveals secrets of occult ritual practice in the Tantric, Hermetic, and Quabbalistic alchemical traditions.

www.herbal-alchemy.com

Made in the USA
San Bernardino, CA
08 January 2016